"I am delighted that a biography of Father Stanley Rother is finally available and that many more people will be introduced to the heroic life and martyrdom of this Servant of God. His witness as a dedicated missionary and pastor is a gift to the Church in our time. María Ruiz Scaperlanda portrays his life with fidelity and warm admiration."

✠ Paul S. Coakley
Archbishop of Oklahoma City

"María Ruiz Scaperlanda has a long and well-deserved reputation as one of our finest Catholic journalists. She is a good storyteller, and she tells the story of Father Stanley Rother with sensitivity and intelligence, introducing us to a holy priest, a defender of the poor, and a missionary martyr of our times — one more shining light in the long history of holiness and heroism in the Americas."

✠ José H. Gomez
Archbishop of Los Angeles

"I am very grateful for this excellently researched biography of a heroic American priest, Father Stanley Rother. He was 'heroic' in his love for his people, a love unto death. This faithful shepherd 'who did not run' was an inspiring example of the priesthood for our seminarians at Mount St. Mary's. With this book, I pray many more seminarians and priests, as well as laity and religious, will be inspired by Father Stan's missionary zeal and love for the poor."

✠ Kevin C. Rhoades
Bishop of Fort Wayne-South Bend
Former Rector of Mount St. Mary's Seminary

"The Church has long been waiting for a clear and concise account of the heroic life and martyrdom of Father Stanley Rother. María Ruiz Scaperlanda's book more than fulfills that need. The author brings to life the faithful Servant of God, whose innate tenacity, devotion to the Church, and unbending fidelity to his flock resulted in a loving and redemptive witness to Christ."

✠ Edward J. Weisenburger
Bishop of Salina, Kansas

"María Ruiz Scaperlanda has done a fine job of drawing on historical and eyewitness sources to paint for us an accurate picture, not only of the events of Father Stanley Rother's ministry and self-sacrificing death for the flock entrusted to his care, but also of Father Rother himself ... a humble, holy, courageous priest who is a true St. John Vianney for our times. This book presents his story in a way that is sure to inspire."

✠ Anthony B. Taylor
Bishop of Little Rock

"Father Stan was a deeply human, eminently relatable man whose struggles and desires will resonate with anyone. To read his story, as is beautifully recounted in this book, is to be reminded that any of us can do great things through God's grace."

Jennifer Fulwiler, radio host and
author of *Something Other Than God*

"Imbued with the values of hard work and community that characterize the American farmland, Father Stanley Rother's life as a missionary priest models for Christians everywhere the powerful effect of grace that is teamed with action and commitment. His eventual martyrdom at the hands of Guatemalan guerrillas is a staggering reminder that a life of holiness, lived for Christ Jesus within a world of hurt, always means a sharing in his cross, his death, and his resurrection. The story of Father Stanley Rother is one that will resonate with Catholics, and with the world, particularly in the age of Pope Francis — a pope of grace and action. María Ruiz Scaperlanda has done a magnificent job of fleshing out a most ordinary man who lived a most extraordinary life, through his willingness to love, as Christ loved."

Elizabeth Scalia, author of *Strange Gods:
Unmasking the Idols in Everyday Life* (Ave Maria Press)
and the upcoming *Little Sins Mean a Lot*
(Our Sunday Visitor, 2016)

"In her tremendous new book, *The Shepherd Who Didn't Run: Father Stanley Rother, Martyr from Oklahoma*, María Ruiz Scaperlanda brings us into close encounter with a heroic priest who will, God willing, soon be a canonized saint. We learn not only of Father Stanley's valiant heroism in the moment of his martyrdom, but also of his life of service to a Church he loved and to her people, who greatly loved him for showing them the path to Christ. Reading this book helps each of us to answer the calling to a life of service in our own unique mission fields. A highly inspirational introduction to an amazing spiritual shepherd."

Lisa M. Hendey, founder of CatholicMom.com
and author of *The Grace of Yes*

"In this edifying and inspiring biography of Father Stanley Rother, priest, missionary, and martyr, the author draws us into the small town of Okarche, Oklahoma, and the village of Santiago Atitlán and unfolds one man's faithful journey. She illustrates how God raises the faithful to the ranks of sanctity and how every small loving act of service deeply impacts lives. A must read."

Donna-Marie Cooper O'Boyle,
EWTN-TV host,
speaker, and award-winning author
of 20 books, including *The Kiss of Jesus*
(www.donnacooperoboyle.com)

"Through vivid description and artful prose, María Ruiz Scaperlanda captures the faith and fortitude of a man who ministered with mercy to people on the margins. This book ensures that the memory of Father Stanley Rother, who gave his life for others, remains alive today."

Kerry Weber, managing editor of
America magazine and author of
Mercy in the City

"The story of Father Stanley Francis Rother's life and death is one that needs to be heard, especially as we witness increasing persecution of our Christian brothers and sisters around the world, and María Ruiz Scaperlanda is just the person to tell this story. From the opening pages, it's obvious that this book is a labor of love — in all the best ways. Thank you, María, for opening our hearts and minds to Father Rother's extraordinary example of faith and trust and love."

Mary DeTurris Poust, retreat leader and author
of six books on Catholic spirituality, including
Everyday Divine: A Catholic Guide to Active Spirituality

"The Holy Spirit reached through the prose of *The Shepherd Who Didn't Run* and into my heart. Father Stanley Rother, an Oklahoma farm boy who gave his life to Christ and died for Christ, was, truly, a Servant of God. Can you imagine a more wonderful title to bear than that? We are all called to be Servants of God, each in the places where he has put us. María Ruiz Scaperlanda writes in clean prose that doesn't get in the way of this story of a priest whom God lifted up to be his witness in life and his martyr in death. Father Rother's story is a beacon pointing to the power of Holy Orders to refine ordinary men into instruments of grace.

"*The Shepherd Who Didn't Run* is destined be a source book on Father Stanley Rother's life. Like the life it shares with us, it is infused with the love of a true priest, a manly man, who lived the Beatitudes and was given the privilege of dying a martyr's death. Father Rother's life and death stand witness to what Jesus intended the priesthood to be when he instituted it in the Upper Room so long ago. *The Shepherd Who Didn't Run* is a testament to his walk with Christ and to the servant priesthood of true priestly vocation that he exemplified."

Former Oklahoma Rep. Rebecca Hamilton,
blogger at Patheos.com
and *National Catholic Register*
(NCRegister.com)

"Father Stanley Rother's love for the people he served pops off the page in this compelling biography by María Ruiz Scaperlanda. With a big heart open both to God and his flock, Rother was the type of priest I want to be and an inspiring Christian witness for our time."

Michael Rossmann, S.J.,
editor in chief of *The Jesuit Post*
(TheJesuitPost.org)

"Compelling! Once I picked up María Ruiz Scaperlanda's *The Shepherd Who Didn't Run*, I could not put it down. Her comprehensive research is expertly woven into a story that is as engaging as it is edifying. Please do not miss out on this incredible piece of work!"

Marge Fenelon, journalist,
speaker, and author of
Imitating Mary and
Our Lady, Undoer of Knots:
A Living Novena

"In taking pen to paper to tell Father Rother's story of sacrificial love, María Ruiz Scaperlanda has achieved something remarkable for God and his people. For in learning of one priest's loyalty toward the '*anawim*' in Guatemala, a world away from the Oklahoma farm of his roots, we cannot help but find our hearts expanded and lurching more fervently toward the Lord of love. Read *The Shepherd Who Didn't Run* with caution, however, for transformation is guaranteed."

Roxane B. Salonen,
the collaborative writer
for Ramona Treviño's story,
Redeemed by Grace:
A Catholic Woman's Journey to
Planned Parenthood and Back

"What words can I use to describe *The Shepherd Who Didn't Run*? Strong, moving, faith-filled, haunting, and so full of the power of God are but a few. María Ruiz Scaperlanda paints a poignant portrait of a man who truly gave it all to God.

"This story of a martyred priest reads quickly and powerfully, as we learn about his early roots and family life, his struggles in the seminary, and ultimately how he ended up in a remote corner of Guatemala, caring deeply for his people. Father Rother's formation as a shepherd unfolds with the turn of each page, drawing us more deeply into his unique mission and ministry.

"This volume is a treasure and should be read by many; I can see it used in both parish book clubs, as well as in catechesis for teens and adults."

Fran Rossi Szpylczyn,
Catholic blogger, writer,
and social media consultant

The
SHEPHERD
Who Didn't Run

Father Stanley Rother,
Martyr from Oklahoma

María Ruiz Scaperlanda

Our Sunday Visitor Publishing Division
Our Sunday Visitor, Inc.
Huntington, IN 46750

To the *many* faithful priests, nuns,
brothers, and sisters who have
— and continue to —
mold and enrich my life.
You are Light!

María Ruiz Scaperlanda
2015, The Year of Consecrated Life

CONTENTS

FOREWORD

In 1981, I learned about the heroic death of Father Stanley Francis Rother. I was then a seminarian at his alma mater, Mount St. Mary's Seminary in Emmitsburg, Maryland. From that time until this day, the witness of Father Rother's life and death has been a source of encouragement and inspiration to me as a seminarian, priest, and now as a bishop. I consider it a great gift of Divine Providence to be entrusted with overseeing the continuation of his cause for beatification and canonization begun by my predecessor, Archbishop Eusebius J. Beltran.

During a visit to Rome in September 2014, it was my privilege to submit the *Positio* concerning Servant of God Father Stanley Rother to Cardinal Angelo Amato, Prefect of the Congregation for the Causes of Saints at the Vatican. A *Positio* is a massive volume representing years of inquiry and the summary of an exhaustive amount of testimony regarding the suitability of someone whose cause for beatification and canonization is being presented to the Holy See.

Father Rother, raised in Okarche, Oklahoma, and ordained in 1963, was a priest of the Archdiocese of Oklahoma City, who, in the manner of the Good Shepherd, laid down his life for the Gospel and for his parishioners. He lived out his priestly vocation as a missionary, serving the parish of Santiago Apóstol (St. James the Apostle), in the Diocese of Sololá-Chimaltenango in Guatemala. He arrived in 1968, served faithfully for thirteen years, and met his violent death on July 28, 1981.

I firmly believe that Father Rother died as a martyr for the faith, and I eagerly await the judgment of the Church concerning his death. It is my ardent hope that he will be declared a martyr and ultimately canonized as a saint, for the glory of God and for the benefit of the universal Church.

At this moment in the history of the Catholic Church, we need attractive models of priestly holiness. We need witnesses to pastoral charity. In the wake of the terrible scandals that have caused such devastation in our Church and in society, the recognition of this generous parish priest's simple manner of life and the sacrificial manner of his death serves as a tremendous affirmation to priests and faithful alike in the United States and around the world.

Here in Oklahoma, where Catholics are a small minority, comprising only 4 to 6 percent of the population, the impact of Father Rother's declaration of martyrdom, beatification, and ultimate canonization would be a powerful spiritual impetus in our efforts in the New Evangelization.

Likewise, in Guatemala, where the Church has suffered bitterly during recent decades in the midst of societal strife, a favorable judgment of martyrdom and subsequent decree of beatification for Father Rother would affirm so many suffering members of the faithful who already esteem Father Rother ("Padre Apla's") as their martyr and saint.

Saints are local. They come from ordinary families, parishes, and communities like Okarche, Oklahoma. But their impact is universal. They belong to the whole Church. They remind us that holiness is our fundamental vocation. Saints represent the full flowering of the grace of our baptism.

I am grateful for this book, the first published biography of Father Stanley Rother. It is my hope that through this work many more people will be inspired by his beautiful life and valiant witness as an icon of Jesus, the Good Shepherd, who did not run.

MOST REVEREND PAUL S. COAKLEY
Archbishop of Oklahoma City

INTRODUCTION

On May 25, 1963, my brother Stanley Francis Rother was ordained as a priest for the then Diocese of Oklahoma City and Tulsa. This following statement was his selection for inscription on his ordination card: "For myself I am a Christian. For the sake of others I am a Priest."

"For Myself I Am a Christian"

Stanley Francis Rother, the eldest, and his four siblings — namely, Elizabeth, James, Carolyn (died in infancy), and Thomas — were raised in a staunchly religious atmosphere, as were most German Catholic families, in the rural settlement of Okarche, Oklahoma, in the late 1930s, '40s, and early '50s. Our family home was literally surrounded by the extended family. Grandparents lived within a mile, and many uncles, aunts, and first and second cousins were within three or four miles, with church and school a little beyond three miles.

This extended family, along with the experiences of the church and school communities, was interlinked with our immediate family in developing a deep faith life and lifelong values indispensable for providing a solid Christian life. The families worshipped at Holy Trinity Church; the children attended Holy Trinity School, from first through twelfth grades, under the tutelage of the Sisters Adorers of the Blood of Christ. Religion classes, daily Mass, sacramental preparation, daily Rosary in the home, and Sunday evening holy hour and benediction, along with other seasonal religious practices were integrated into our daily lives. Our Christian values were indeed formed by the people with whom we associated, and we certainly had some of the best!

"Come and Follow Me" (see Mt 4:19)

For the 18 formative years of his life, Stanley was absorbed in the security of his family, church, and school. When he journeyed to the seminary some 500 miles away, he took with him his faith, his values, his prayer life, and the prayers of others, but left behind the network of people and practices that had supported him, encouraged him, and nourished him. Armed with this deep faith life and a strong value system, Stanley now embarked on the next phase of his life.

Only after I recently read from the diaries that he kept in those first few years in the seminary did I realize how the religious practices from his home life continued to be so important to him. I was even more surprised to read that he was experiencing such challenging struggles in his studies. Though he had these unexpected academic challenges during this time, I believe he became stronger for it. Stan was a man of prayer; he had an unwavering desire to be a priest, and he believed and trusted that in God he would find his way.

"For the Sake of Others I Am a Priest"

As I reflected on Stanley's 51st anniversary this year, I remembered the many family, friends, and hometown parishioners who joyfully gathered for his ordination at the Cathedral of Our Lady of Perpetual Help in Oklahoma City. But how could we know that in 18 years most of these same friends and relatives would again gather in Our Lady's cathedral, this time for his funeral Mass.

Father Stanley's first four years following ordination were spent serving as an assistant in four different parishes in Oklahoma, which involved a variety of ministerial duties and activities. Periodically, I would receive a letter from him, usually sharing a bit about the parish where he was serving and what he was doing. He was always positive and obviously enjoyed his work, except for the time he shared his woes about trying to keep his elementary-school religion classes under control: "Would you please give me some ideas I could try?" Since, as a teacher myself, I had some experience in that area, I shared a few hints with him.

In the spring of 1967, Father Stanley made the request of his bishop to serve as a missionary priest in the parish of Santiago Apóstol (St. James the Apostle), in the town of Santiago Atitlán, Guatemala, site of the Oklahoma-sponsored mission. After some deliberation, the bishop granted the request. Thus, that summer Father Stan literally left all that was familiar — including family, friends, food, language, the red dirt of Oklahoma — packed his pickup with supplies the missionaries in Santiago had requested, and headed south (some 2,500 miles) to his new parish, his new beginning.

"God's Flock Is in Your Midst; Give It a Shepherd's Care" (1 Pt 5:2)

Stan incurred unexpected realities as he gradually found his niche with his co-workers and among the people with whom he was destined to serve. Obviously, he possessed hidden reserves of an inner strength, convictions and a deep faith that motivated him to succeed. Learning to understand and speak the languages of the people, both Spanish and Tz'utujil, were noteworthy accomplishments for him. Because of Stan's ability to converse with the people in their native languages, there was an increased involvement with them, in their sacramental life, liturgies, and family life. He visited the elderly and sick in their homes and learned and appreciated their customs. Stan's identification with the people of Santiago Atitlán was not difficult for him, because of the simplicity of lifestyle he himself embraced.

A Glimpse of My Brother
as a Priest and Missionary

I was blessed with the opportunity to spend two different summers, 1972 and 1975, working at the mission with Father Stan and three sisters from my religious community, the Sisters Adorers of the Blood of Christ. These summers contained a cache of treasured memories for me, as our time together as adults had been very limited due to our ministries. To observe his relationship with the parishioners, how comfortable he was in his surroundings, and his dealing with many unexpected events throughout a day was a precious gift to me.

It was most rewarding to me to see Stan in different roles of his ministry: celebrating liturgies was special, going to the market, showing some young men how to fix the truck that wasn't running, fixing an electrical problem in the hospital, working on the farm with the men, having fun with the children, visiting the elderly or sick in their homes, burying someone's loved one, and myriad other activities. So obvious to me was his gentleness, his truly being for others (not just doing for them), and his attentiveness and responsiveness to them when he was locked in conversation. I was not prepared for what I experienced or the conditions of his surroundings I observed, but my appreciation, gratitude, and pride for my brother rose to a new level.

Though Stan was busy with his own duties much of the time, and I was kept busy helping the sisters in their work, we did find opportunities to get away for a "day off." I most always went with him each week to at least one of the outlying little churches where he had Mass. Sometimes we had to take the mountain roads, which had steep drop-offs and were narrow and downright scary. One of the first times on such a trip he wryly remarked, "If we start sliding off, jump out!"

One afternoon we walked about a mile up the mountain to a location from which we had a beautiful view of Lake Atitlán, the towering volcanic mountain San Pedro behind it, and the village below us. The beauty of the landscape was breathtaking; the poverty below us was heartbreaking. This place was, for Stan, a place of quiet, a sacred place where he would retreat on occasion to renew his spiritual and physical energies in communing with his God. I truly felt honored that he shared this sacred place with me. I knew that this was not his first time to this site, and I know that it was not his last. The whole experience on this mountain site was for me worth the tedious trek up the mountainside, and peacefulness of mind and heart I received.

It continues to challenge me to know that my brother, an ordinary person like you or like me, could give himself in the prime of his life to such a complete dedication to serve "the poorest of the poor" of another culture and language, and to give of himself in such an extraordinary way. All of which led to "the shepherd who didn't run."

SISTER MARITA ROTHER, A.S.C.
September 2015

CHAPTER 1

Love to the Extreme Limit

July 28, 1981: The Shepherd Who Didn't Run

It was a quiet, clear night in the lakeside village of Santiago Atitlán. For almost a week now, the moderate, cool temperatures in the Guatemala highlands had been chilly enough for a jacket in the middle of summer.

Sounds travel far in this isolated region of Guatemala, where the only recurring nighttime noises are animal ones. No sound of A/C units. No sound of cars and highways. No planes flying overhead or trains nearby. The type of silence experienced by most people in the United States only when camping in the deep woods, during a storm blackout, or by someone living in farm country. It was a silence well familiar to Stanley Francis Rother, a native of Okarche, Oklahoma.

The sound of three men breaking into the rectory of St. James the Apostle Church at 1:30 a.m. must have carried well beyond the village square — their enraged voices and aggressive movements like nails hammering a public message of terror to any listening ear.

Wearing civilian clothes and ski masks, the three Spanish-speaking Ladinos (non–indigenous men), were familiar enough with the parish complex to know the precise location of the pastor's upstairs bedroom. They rushed there first but found no one in the room.

Then across the hall they seized Francisco Bocel, the 19-year-old brother of the associate pastor, who had been working at the rectory and staying there provisionally. They put a gun to the terrified young man's head and threatened to kill him if he did not take them to the pastor immediately.

Francisco led the attackers down the stairs and to the door of a corner utility room. He knocked, calling out in terror, "Padre, they've come for you."

That's when Father Stanley, aware of the danger to the young man, opened the door and let his killers in. Francisco was ordered to go back upstairs to his room and lock the door, and he did so — remaining there for the next 20 minutes.

The assailants wanted to kidnap Father Stanley, turn him into one of the *desaparecidos* (the missing). But he would have none of that. He was aware of Francisco, of the nine unsuspecting sisters in the convent across the patio, and of the other innocents in the rectory that night — all in danger of also being dragged away. And Father Stanley knew they would torture and, ultimately, kill him. He never called for help.

From his hiding place, Francisco heard the muffled noises of a struggle — bodies crashing into furniture and each other, several thuds. There was a gunshot. Then another. Then silence, followed by the sound of scrambling feet running away. After what seemed an endless period of silence, Francisco found the courage to come out of his hiding space. He rushed to wake up Bertha Sánchez, a nurse volunteer staying in the parish complex, and he ran to alert the Carmelite sisters in the convent across the courtyard from the rectory. "They killed him! They killed Padre Francisco!"

The women ran in and found Father Stanley shot in the head and lying in a pool of his blood. They immediately began to pray. His dear friend Bertha pronounced Stanley Francis Rother dead at the scene.

The Santiago Atitlán Mission: A Return to Ministry

How a 46-year-old priest from a small German farming community in Oklahoma came to live and die in this remote, ancient Guatemalan village is a story full of wonder and God's providence.

When Pope St. John XXIII requested in the early 1960s that North Americans send missionaries to South and Central America, the Oklahoma Church responded.

In 1964, the then Diocese of Oklahoma City and Tulsa took over the care of the church of St. James the Apostle (Santiago Apóstol), the heart of the oldest parish in the Diocese of Sololá, dating back to the 16th century. But no resident priest had served the indigenous Tz'utujil community of Santiago Atitlán for almost a century. Oklahoma priests, sisters, and lay workers served the mission until 2000, when sufficient growth in local vocations allowed the Guatemala diocese, now called the Diocese of Sololá-Chimaltenango, to resume pastoral care.

From the onset, that first Oklahoma missionary team understood that the Tz'utujil are an agricultural people who retain much of their ancient Mayan culture and pride. This was a perfect fit for Father Stanley, a farming boy from the western Oklahoma town of Okarche.

When he arrived at Santiago Atitlán in 1968, Father Stanley instantly fell in love with the volatile and stunning land of volcanoes and earthquakes — but above all, with its people. His Tz'utujil Indian parishioners called him "Padre Apla's," which translates as "Francis" or "Francisco" in the native Tz'utujil language. When speaking in Spanish, they called Father Stanley "Padre Francisco," based on "Francis," his middle name, because it was easier to pronounce than the Spanish for Stanley, "Estanislao." Over his years of service, Father Stanley helped develop a farmers' co-op, a nutrition center, a school, a hospital clinic, and the first Catholic radio station in the area, which was used for catechesis.

And although he did not institute the project, he was a critical driving force in developing Tz'utujil as a written language, which led to translations of the liturgy of the Mass and the Lectionary, with the New Testament in Tz'utujil being published after his death.

In the most tangible way, Father Stan exemplified with his life and through his vocation what Pope Francis described regarding the distinctive ministry of men and women who choose a consecrated life: "A radical approach is required of all Christians, but religious persons are called upon to follow the Lord in a special way: They are men and women who can awaken the world."

"Consecrated life is prophecy," Pope Francis emphasized. "God asks us to fly the nest and to be sent to the frontiers of the world, avoiding the temptation to 'domesticate' them. This is the most concrete way of imitating the Lord."[1]

"If It Is My Destiny That I Should Give My Life Here, Then So Be It ..."

Once Guatemala's civil war found its way to the peaceful villages surrounding beautiful Lake Atitlán, many people, like Father Stanley's own catechists, began to disappear regularly.

Father Stanley's response was to show his people the way of love and peace with his life. He walked the roads looking for the bodies of the dead, to bring them home for a proper burial, and he fed the widows and orphans of those killed or "disappeared."

In a letter dated September 1980 to the bishops of Tulsa and Oklahoma City, Father Stanley described the political and anti-Church climate in Guatemala:

> The reality is that we are in danger. But we don't know when or what form the government will use to further repress the Church.... Given the situation, I am not ready to leave here just yet. There is a chance that the Govt. will back off. If I get a direct threat or am told to leave, then I will go. But if it is my destiny that I should give my life here, then so be it.... I don't want to desert these people, and that is what will be said, even after all these years. There is still a lot of good that can be done under the circumstances.

In his final Christmas letter to Oklahoma Catholics published in two diocesan newspapers that same year, he once again concluded: "The shepherd cannot run at the first sign of danger. Pray for us that we may be a sign of the love of Christ for our people, that our presence among them will fortify them to endure these sufferings in preparation for the coming of the Kingdom."[2]

But a month later, and six months before his death, Father Stanley and his associate pastor left Guatemala under threat of death after witnessing the abduction of a parish catechist. However, he returned to his beloved Guatemala in time to celebrate

Holy Week in April of 1981, ignoring the pleas of those who urged him to consider his own safety.

On July 12, 1981, in a statement read in all the nation's parishes, the Guatemalan bishops denounced "a carefully studied plan" by the government "to intimidate the Church and silence its prophetic voice."

"Just before he returned to Guatemala for the last time, he told me how much he desired to come back," recalled Archbishop Emeritus Eusebius J. Beltran, in a 30th-anniversary message to the community of Cerro de Oro, one of the mission's satellite churches near Santiago Atitlán.

"He knew the dangers that existed here at that time and was greatly concerned about the safety and security of the people. Despite these threats and danger, he returned and resumed his great priestly ministry to you.... It is very clear that Padre Apla's died for you and for the faith," said Archbishop Beltran, who served as bishop of Tulsa in 1981 when Father Rother was killed.

As We Get Started

During his seminary years in San Antonio, Stanley struggled in his studies, even failing his first year of theology. When the seminary suggested that he should consider a different vocation, Stanley requested another chance, and the supportive bishop agreed. He successfully completed his studies at Mount St. Mary's Seminary in Emmitsburg, Maryland.

Father Stanley served the first five years of his priestly ministry without much notice in various Oklahoma assignments. But everything changed when he answered the call to serve at the mission in Guatemala, a decision that led him to find his heart's vocation as a priest to the Tz'utujil people.

This farmer from Okarche, Oklahoma, who loved the land and recognized God in all of creation, was never afraid to dig in and get his own hands dirty — a trait deeply loved by his Tz'utujil people.

Certainly the fact that Father Stanley's route to the priesthood was a difficult one only emphasizes the reality that his desire to serve the People of God as their priest never wavered. Over and over, both in his native Oklahoma and his adopted Guatemala, the stories involving Father Stanley highlight his unassuming, hard-working ethic, a perseverance he was known to execute all the way to stubborn!

Almost 35 years after his martyrdom, Father Rother is more than remembered by the parish community in Santiago Atitlán. The faithful devotion of the people make it clear that Padre Francisco is *still* witnessing the presence and power of God to his people.

From one generation to the next, the men and women of Santiago Atitlán continue to tell the story about the gringo from Oklahoma who became one of them: the priest who loved them, worked with them, stood up for them, and was even willing to die with them.

In a very real way, Father Stanley remains *their* priest.

As the stories of those who knew him will verify here, Father Stanley's single-minded devotion was to living and embodying the Love of God he himself experienced — a Love that he believed with his whole heart was his mission to proclaim, in word and action, to all of humanity.

In my biography *Edith Stein: St. Teresa Benedicta of the Cross*, I quoted Edith Stein as declaring, "Pure spirits are like rays

of light through which the eternal light communes with creation....To believe in saints means only to sense in them God's
presence."[3]

Father Stanley was a pure spirit, one of 13 priests — and the
first American priest — slain during Guatemala's 36-year guerrilla war, a tragedy that ultimately claimed an estimated total
of 140,000 lives. This text is not meant to be a comprehensive
collection or a definitive presentation on his life, or his death, or
his cause for canonization. This book is meant to honor the faith
and faithfulness of Stanley Francis Rother — Padre Apla's — a
brilliant ray of light in the midst of a very dark period in the
history of Guatemala and the Americas.

"Who are martyrs? They are Christians who have been
'earned' by Christ, disciples who have learnt well the sense of
that 'love to the extreme limit' which led Jesus to the Cross,"
Pope Francis remarked in October 2013, on the beatification of
522 Spanish martyrs who were killed during the anti-Christian
persecutions of the 1930s.

"There is no such thing as love in installments, no such thing
as portions of love. Total love: and when we love, we love till the
end.

"On the Cross, Jesus felt the weight of death, the weight of
sin, but he gave himself over to the Father entirely, and he for-
gave. He barely spoke, but he gave the gift of life," Pope Francis
continued. "Christ 'beats' us in love; the martyrs imitated him
in love until the very end.... We implore the intercession of the
martyrs, that we may be concrete Christians, Christians in deeds
and not just in words, that we may not be mediocre Christians, Christians painted in a superficial coating of Christianity
without substance — they weren't painted, they were Christians

until the end. We ask them for help in keeping our faith firm, that even throughout our difficulties we may nourish hope and foster brotherhood and solidarity."[4]

There was nothing "painted" in Stanley, the young man who chose to follow Jesus as his disciple:

- Stanley, the seminarian who endured difficulties, even failure, yet persevered in his calling to the priesthood;

- Father Stanley, the young parish priest who put aside his fears, courageously agreeing to serve the People of God in Oklahoma's mission in Guatemala;

- Father Stanley, the man who struggled to pass Latin and learn Spanish, yet succeeded in learning the rare and challenging Mayan dialect of his Tz'utujil parishioners;

- Father Stanley, the Okarche farmer who believed plowing the fields manually next to the Tz'utujil farmers was part of his vocation as a minister of God's love;

- And finally, Father Stanley, the shepherd who chose to face death rather than abandon his flock — the shepherd who didn't run.

It is my hope and my prayer that in the telling of Father Stanley's story I succeed in introducing you to one person who loved "to the extreme limit," as Pope Francis described, in making God's presence real, tangible to the people in his life — by living, loving, and being himself completely.

To paraphrase the question asked in the Gospels by incredulous people about Jesus of Nazareth: can anything good come from Okarche, Oklahoma? I invite you to come and see.

May the farmer from Okarche inspire you as he has me!

—

What we call the beginning is often the end
And to make an end is to make a beginning.
The end is where we start from….

We shall not cease from exploration
And the end of all our exploring
Will be to arrive where we started
And know the place for the first time.

> — T. S. Eliot, *Four Quartets*,
> Quartet No. 4:
> "Little Gidding," Section V

CHAPTER 2

Son of the Red Earth State

Originally within the Cheyenne-Arapaho Nation, Stanley Rother's hometown of Okarche developed around the train depot constructed by the Chicago, Kansas and Nebraska Railway. It built its Kansas-Texas line through the area in 1890 — only one year after a land run on the "Unassigned Lands" had established Oklahoma City.

Two years later, the 1892 opening of the Cheyenne-Arapaho territories to non-Indian settlement brought a sudden rush of eager settlers to what became the town of Okarche, a name created from the first letters of Oklahoma, Arapaho, and Cheyenne.

It is not difficult to imagine why Stanley Rother's German farming ancestors would have been attracted to owning and cultivating land in the 3.5 million acres suddenly opened for the taking in Oklahoma territory.

A Long Lineage of Germans, Farmers, Catholics

In 1893, 31-year-old Frank Emil Rother and his wife, Gertrude Giefer, Stanley Rother's paternal great-grandparents, arrived in Oklahoma from Minnesota and bought the land near Okarche, where Stanley would be born and raised. Frank Emil, who anglicized his name from Franz when he emigrated from Prussia at the age of 16, came to America with his parents and five of his siblings — all of whom had settled in or around New Trier, Minnesota.

When Frank Emil and Gertrude announced their plans to leave Minnesota and move to the newly opened territory known for its iron-rich red dirt, they shocked the rest of the Rother clan — who resorted to disastrous predictions of their future to scare them into staying: "The Indians will kill you" and "You'll never make it, you'll be back."

It didn't work. Frank Emil and Gertrude, along with their four children, as well as Gertrude's mother and stepfather, left Minnesota for the unfamiliar territory of Oklahoma, traveling by train. Their furniture, farm equipment, and even their horses were carefully arranged in a boxcar. Frank Emil is still described in family lore by his stamina and physical strength — and is remembered for his ethic of hard work.

In 1910, the oldest son of Frank Emil and Gertrude, Frank A., wed Elizabeth Schlecht at Holy Trinity Church in Okarche. Within a year, Elizabeth gave birth to their first child and named him Franz, continuing the long Rother family tradition of naming their firstborn in honor of St. Francis. He would one day be Stanley's father.

Stanley's maternal ancestors — the Schmitts — also emigrated from Germany, leaving Trier in 1843 for Johnsburg, Illinois — what is now a village in northwest suburban Chicago. In thanksgiving for surviving the treacherous voyage across the Atlantic, Frederick Schmitt built a small white chapel dedicated to the Virgin Mary. The building still stands today, alongside what is now Chapel Hill Road. It is maintained by descendants of the Schmitt family.

Frederick Schmitt (later anglicized as Smith) married Wisconsin-native Anna Ottis in October 1882. Around the same time, the Schmitts moved from Illinois to an all-German settlement in St. Bernard Township, Nebraska, about 80 miles northwest of Omaha.

Then, around 1902, the Schmitt family relocated to western Oklahoma. The second of their 10 children was John K. Schmitt (by then, Smith), who married Mary Werner on October 10, 1907. They were blessed with a dozen children, the fourth of whom was named Gertrude Katherine Smith (Stanley's mother), born in 1913.

The Schmitts/Smiths, like the Rothers, were farmers — and devoted Catholics, active in the daily life of Holy Trinity Church in Okarche.

Becoming Oklahomans

On November 29, 1933, Franz A. Rother married Gertrude Katherine Smith, and she soon thereafter gave birth to Stanley Francis Rother — the first of five children.

The year Stanley was born, the Rother family farm was one of 213,325 working farms in the state of Oklahoma, historically the peak year for family and tenant farming. But it was a tough place and time to be a farmer. Not only was the country still recovering from the market crash and the Great Depression, but Oklahoma and the Great Plains had also been hit hard with terrible drought and horrendous dust storms, creating what became known as the Dust Bowl.

The town of Okarche, founded two years before Oklahoma became a state in 1907, now boasted a population that hovered around 450 people, most of them German by birth or descendants of German immigrants, like Stanley's family.

In a 1995 interview with historian Father David Monahan, Franz Rother, Stanley's father, remembered the division between English speakers and German speakers. In his family, Franz grew up speaking German, and he even took German his first four years at school at Holy Trinity. "If my dad would catch us kids talking English," Franz noted, "he would say, 'Don't you kids know how to speak?!'"

For the Catholic community, bilingual services were the norm. Following the tradition of their pastor Monsignor Zenon Steber, when someone met a priest or a sister in Okarche, they would first salute them with the words, "Praised be Jesus Christ" (in German). Monsignor Steber's homilies at Holy Trinity Church were in both German and English.

According to Franz, there was a big department store in town called "Hau-Eischen," an L-shaped building that wrapped around the bank and fronted on Main Street. The department store stood at the site of what is now Eischen's, the oldest bar in Oklahoma — and famous for its secret-recipe fried chicken. When Stanley was born, U.S. Route 81, a fully paved federal highway, ran through the township of Okarche. By the time he turned four, the Northwest Highway (OK-3), connecting Oklahoma City and Okarche, was opened as a gravel-surfaced road.

The Rother Family

Born on March 27, 1935, in the midst of a western Oklahoma dust storm, Stanley Francis Rother grew up instinctively connected to the land — and the land he belonged to was grand, made up of big, expansive skies, and miles and miles of rolling prairie visible in every direction.

Although Franz and Gertrude named him Stanley in honor of the many relatives in Gertrude's lineage named Stanislaus, when it came time for his baptism two days after he was born, Monsignor Steber would not baptize the baby boy unless his first name was Francis, continuing the family tradition of naming their first boy after St. Francis of Assisi.

But in spite of his baptism record stating it otherwise, to his extensive family and other friends, he was always Stanley.

Franz and Gertrude's family grew quickly. On May 24, 1936, 14 months after Stanley, Elizabeth Mary (Betty Mae, now Sister Marita) was born. A year later, James Henry (Jim) was born on July 13, 1937. The following year tragedy struck the family when a baby girl, Carolyn Ann, was born on November 10, 1938, and she unexpectedly died the next day. Two years later, on June 2, 1940, Thomas Joseph was born. With four children under the age of five, life in the Rother farmhouse must have been busy and full of life.

In 1933, shortly before he and Gertrude Smith were married, Franz Rother made his first payment on their house. Built in 1918, this house where the five Rother children were born and raised is now home to their son Tom and his wife, Marti, and their family. Until the 1950s, the house had no running water. A pump in the screened-in porch off the kitchen was their source of drinking water. A bucket of water with a dipper for all to use was on a kitchen cabinet. The cook stove burned coal and wood, which meant that in the winter the kitchen became the center of all family activity, including daily homework around the table.

"Of course we didn't know these were inconveniences while we were growing up. It was the same for everyone else we knew," reflected Sister Marita. "Most of the money that people had back then went into the farmland," Tom added, smiling. "As long as doors shut and the windows opened, everything was okay."

The Rother family never thought of themselves as being poor, except perhaps when the wheat crop was hailed out or, as Tom remembered, "the year the drought hit and we could cut wheat all day and we wouldn't fill a truck." But the number of good years in between kept farmers hopeful from year to year.

The large family garden could be watered from the tall windmill close to the barn, Sister Marita explained, and it provided much fresh produce for their meals in the summer months. Countless hours were spent canning enough vegetables, fruit, and meat to get them through the cold winter months. Raising chickens and milk cows provided the family with milk, cream, butter, eggs, and meat. Money from selling eggs and cream at the grocery store, recalled the Rother siblings, helped them to buy necessities like flour, sugar, rice, cocoa, and other condiments. With these they were able to have homemade bread, cinnamon rolls, pies, and cakes. "Our mother was the best cook and baker!" said Tom and Sister Marita.

According to Stanley's first biographer, Father David Monahan,* a favorite memory of Gertrude about her oldest son took place on an ordinary afternoon as the family feasted on watermelon. After the group went back to work, discarding

---

* Father David Monahan wrote the first biography of Father Stanley Rother. It remains unpublished. See "Acknowledgments" for more information.

the watermelon rinds outside, Gertrude had a good laugh at the sight of a young Stan in the yard with a rind encircling his neck.

By the age of five, each of the Rother children joined in the work of the farm, with specific chores assigned to each one. The younger ones helped collect eggs and feed the chickens, and by age eight, everyone milked the cows. The family had five or six milk cows, and they had to be milked twice daily: at 6:30 in the morning and at 5:00 in the evening. This took 30 to 45 minutes, including separating the milk from the cream. On school days, this meant wearing old clothes for chores, then changing into overalls for the boys and a dress for Sister Marita before going to school.

Stanley began driving the family tractor when he was 10 years old, and it became obvious from the beginning that he excelled at learning and working with anything that required mechanical know-how. His father, Franz, liked to tell the story of how he "rigged up a safety belt" for Stanley when he began to drive the tractor, in order to keep him from falling off the tractor seat and being run over by a disc plow or other device.

In spite of tough conditions, Tom remembered with pride being about nine years old and going out with his big brother to do chores, check the ponds — and cut the wheat. "I drove the truck, and Stan would push up and dump the wheat into it. I'd start the truck and move it to another terrace so that he could dump into it. There wasn't anything that Stan wouldn't tackle," Tom added with admiration. "And he could pretty well fix just about anything."

To this day, Sister Marita remembers vividly the moments when kid's play blended into family chores and duties. There's the time when Jim, Stanley, and Sister Marita carried out their assigned chore of collecting eggs — and then proceeded to make mud pies with several eggs behind the chicken house. It was all great fun until that evening when their mother made a chocolate cake for dessert, and the kids didn't get any because, as she told them, "Yours is out behind the chicken house."

Or the time that Stanley keenly observed his sister as she carefully propped her mystery novel over the sink in order to steal a few lines of reading while she washed or dried the dishes. Hours later, when he knew she'd be reading in her bedroom, as Sister Marita intensely focused on the story line of *Murder in the Nunnery*, Stanley sneaked down the hall and shouted in front of her open door — making Sister Marita scream and her book go flying high.

"Stanley is a tease, in little things," she laughed, remembering that story. "He is 14 months older than I am," she added, unaware of using the present tense. "We are very close."

For the Rothers in Okarche, experiencing the extended family took on a whole new meaning since they lived among their relatives. You could walk across a field and be at a relative's house, Sister Marita described. Like any other siblings, the foursome got along well — though they had the normal sibling fights. She remembered once in the flare of a fight throwing a tin can at Stanley. "I was scared to death when I saw he was bleeding." The can cut him above an eye, giving him a small scar for the rest of his life.

Life for the Rothers centered on the family, the farm, and the Church and its traditions. From an early age, Stanley and his siblings learned the importance of prayer and praying together as a family. Whether to attend church on Sunday was never a question. And learning what it meant to live the Catholic faith and its practices was an everyday affair, such as kneeling by their chairs around the kitchen table after supper to pray the Rosary.

"We prayed a lot together as a family, and I know that's what drew us closer," Sister Marita explained. "During meals we carried on a conversation — except for one night a week when my parents liked to listen to a program on the radio called 'The Squeaking Door' [*Inner Sanctum Mysteries* show]," she said, laughing. "I didn't like that, so I busied myself doing other things."

Perhaps like many German families, the Rothers were not "touchy-feely," as youngest brother Tom explained it. And they didn't take time to talk a whole lot about emotions or personal things. He described Stanley, in particular, as being "so quiet. It was hard to carry on a conversation unless one really worked at it. You had to pump and to pump!"

Even a decision as significant as going to the seminary — or to the convent — was not a public topic for discussion. So when Stanley graduated from high school and Sister Marita decided to leave for the convent at the end of her junior year, the brother and sister were shocked to find out that they were both moving away at the same time.

"No, I didn't talk to him about it. And I didn't know he was going to the seminary. We didn't feel the need to discuss it, evidently," Sister Marita said, smiling.

School: A Family Competition

In 1941, Stanley Francis Rother began first grade at Holy Trinity Catholic School, beginning the string of little Rothers that the nuns liked to describe as "the three little bears," all one year apart.

Harold Wittrock, his cousin and classmate from first grade through high school, described Stanley as "an average all-American boy who participated in all the functions of school as a normal boy. Stan was real sincere. Whatever his potential was, he did everything with his abilities to be the best he could. He never sloughed off. He wasn't a quitter."

All the Rother children attended the two-storied red brick Holy Trinity Catholic School, from first grade through high school. The primary grades were located in the basement of the building. The intermediate grades were on the first floor. And the high school took over the top floor.

Sister Marita still remembers being competitive in her family, especially with Stanley. In their small Holy Trinity School, where two grades often shared one room, this meant the brother and sister were frequently together in one classroom: "I think all of us were pretty good students. We were expected to do well in school."

At the same time, she also remembers Stanley looking out for her as early as grade school. "I won't say he was a protector, but he did make sure that I was okay. He looked after me in school, and he did that even after we were grown. In his letters, he would always ask, 'How's everything going? Are you happy in what you're doing? How's life treating you?' "

Most of Stanley's teachers at Holy Trinity were sisters from the Adorers of the Blood of Christ religious community, based in Wichita, Kansas.

His second-grade teacher at Okarche, Sister Flora Jentgen, A.S.C., described Stanley as "alert, average, always polite," noting that he became "embarrassed when others were too noisy. He was a real boy." Sister Flora, who was at Holy Trinity for two years, also remembered seven-year-old Stanley as "kind, unassuming, and deeply caring."

Sister Agatha Wassinger, A.S.C., taught third and fourth grades in one classroom at Holy Trinity, so she had Stanley and Sister Marita together. She described Stanley as "a good child" who she never had to correct. "I think studying was a little hard, but he worked like a trooper." One story about Stanley that she's never forgotten was the day a doctor came to give immunization shots to the students. When Stanley saw the needle, "he turned pale. For just a second, he kind of passed out. He was so embarrassed."

Stanley's cousin and classmate Harold shared with him a passion for vocational agriculture activities during high school. "He showed steers. I showed pigs," Harold remembered. Stanley was elected president of the Future Farmers of America during his senior year. "We showed our livestock at the Oklahoma City fair, and Stan won some prizes with his steers."

Harold also described an embarrassing incident, during that same event in Oklahoma City, when he, Stanley, and other Okarche boys were caught being mischievous. "We were walking down the midway. We'd seen one of these girlie shows. As we were going up the ramp, there was a minister of a church in Okarche looking at us!"

Classmate Mary Jane Schwarz, who became Sister Denise, once she joined the Adorers of the Blood of Christ, said that Stanley was thought of as an average student academically. "He was quiet, reserved, but still kind of ornery. He always had a twinkle in his eye when he was up to something."

Holy Trinity School and parish encouraged the students to take advantage of and participate in as many activities as their farm chores would allow — and the options were many, especially opportunities to grow in the Catholic faith. Stanley, for example, was trained by Monsignor Zenon Steber, his pastor, to be an altar server when he was only eight years old — and continued to serve until graduation from high school. In addition to daily Mass at eight o'clock every morning, the school held an annual retreat for its students. The high school yearbook for 1953, the year Stanley graduated, was dedicated to Our Lady of Fátima.

Along with his family duties, Stanley pursued a myriad of interests in high school: he was on the basketball team, first as a player and then as a manager; in Future Farmers of America, becoming FFA president his senior year; and in drama, including a title role in *Don't Take My Penny*. Stanley was also involved in the movement Young Christian Students and in the Sodality of Our Lady, an association that fostered devotion to the Blessed Virgin Mary.

Stanley did not struggle academically in high school. In fact, he had only one low mark of a D, in religion, the first semester of his sophomore year. He graduated sixth in the class of 22 students.

They were a close-knit group who "ran around together" in high school, Mary Jane remembered. "We did a lot of things as a group. Stan and I wrote to each other, even while he was in Guatemala." When Mary Jane entered religious life, Stan attended her reception and profession into the Adorers of the Blood of Christ.

Emalene Reherman Schwarz was one of a handful of young women who dated Stanley Rother in high school. A lot of the social activities, however, were done as a group. On weekend nights, for example, Emalene recalled how a group would come together to drive to the Highway 81 Cafe, 10 miles away in the larger town of Kingfisher. But if it was a Friday, she explained, the teens would wait until after midnight to have their hamburgers.

According to Emalene, Stanley was not particularly shy around girls. She remembered that Stanley's locker was next to hers at school, and he had "a nice smile" and laughed easily. "He was a nice, quiet, pleasant person to be around, an enjoyable person, a warm person." Physically, Stanley's high school transcript described him as 5 feet, 10 inches tall, weighing a lean 162 pounds, with brown hair and eyes.

In the 1950s, and in this agricultural setting, it was a reliable assumption that boys would become farmers after they graduated from high school and that most girls would marry a farmer. In fact, only four people in their graduating class entered college, and of those four, three of them were religious vocations.

Needless to say, religious vocations were dynamically promoted by the sisters at the school and by the pastors at Holy Trinity. But they were also promoted by Oklahoma's Bishop Eugene McGuinness, whose well-known motto was, "You've given me your money, now give me your flesh and blood!"

By 1953, four men from Okarche had been ordained priests and approximately 40 women had entered the Sisters Adorers of the Blood of Christ.

Looking back on their years growing up together in such a close community of families, many of whom were relatives as well as friends, Stanley's classmates are especially touched that the only official reunion of the class of 1953 took place when Stanley was ordained. Franz and Gertrude Rother reserved seats for the classmates to attend and celebrate together Father Stanley Rother's first Mass.

Stanley's Road to the Priesthood:
A Vision of Mission

The man who was Stanley's first model of priestly ministry was Father Zenon Steber, a native of Alsace-Lorraine and former missionary. At the age of 22, Father Steber left everything he knew to serve as a priest in the tropical Gold Coast, modern-day Ghana. Although he was forced to return home after contracting a serious illness, Father Steber didn't deter from his call to serve as a missionary priest — this time applying to Bishop Theophile Meerschaert, the vicar apostolic of Indian Territory, including the Oklahoma Territory.

When Father Steber was assigned to Okarche in 1903, it was clear from the start who was in charge. A short and stout man, Father Steber was by all accounts a commanding presence in the Catholic community at Okarche. Yet stories about his strict rules regarding the code of behavior at church and school are balanced by his personal interaction with the people.

Emalene Reherman, Stanley's classmate and lifelong friend, admitted that as a child she was afraid of Father Steber's strict and stern demeanor. There was a reason that misbehaving children were sent to Father Steber. The altar servers got a special dose of discipline, especially during Mass when he'd call altar servers "*Dummkopf!*" if they missed a cue. But Emalene also knew that "his heart was in the place of being a good priest."

By the time Stanley was born, Holy Trinity pastor Father Steber had become a monsignor. And it was with this missionary priest that Stanley first experienced the sacraments and liturgy: his baptism, First Communion, confirmation, and reconciliation.

In the years when she was still called Betty Mae, Sister Marita remembered Monsignor Steber's strictness, but also how much he loved being around the kids. "I remember him coming by my desk and taking long curls from each side and tying them together under my chin," she said. "When he'd be on the playground, we would all run and want to be around him."

In truth, we have no way to know how much Stanley took in and incorporated Monsignor Steber's discipline, style, or French gentility. But it is safe to say that his first pastor must have influenced him deeply in his 12 years of schooling before heading to the seminary.

Perhaps the missionary spirit of Monsignor Steber even instilled in Stanley a more global and inclusive experience of the Catholic Church and its vocation to service and mission, one more expansive than Stanley would have known otherwise, growing up in Oklahoma's farm country.

There were two other men who would directly influence Stanley's image of the priesthood in Okarche: Father Edmund Von Elm and Father Camille Boesmans.

Father Von Elm was assigned as a pastor to Okarche in 1947 when Monsignor Steber became seriously ill. The young American pastor became a good friend of the Franz and Gertrude Rother family and spent a lot of time visiting, dining, and even working in the fields with the Rother men.

And Father Camille Boesmans, a young Belgian missionary who had been expelled from China, was assigned as associate pastor to Holy Trinity Church, ministering to the school and the parish during the four years that Stanley was in high school.

In essence, 18-year-old Stanley might have never traveled the world, but the world — and, in particular, the understanding of unity and service to the universal Catholic Church — had been brought home to him.

I Want to Be a Priest

When you open Holy Trinity Catholic School's 1953 yearbook, the first photo is not of the school but of the exterior of the church. Above the church picture is the sentence: "Daily Mass is the Source of Strength to live for God, to serve the neighbor, to merit for heaven."

As Father Monahan writes in his biography of Stanley Rother, "To a Catholic youngster sensitive to color, design and symbolism, as Stanley's later life would reveal, the old-fashioned church must have been a good teacher."[5]

Stanley would have been conscious of his family's deep and profound Catholic roots in this church and community. The side altar on the north side of the church was the gift of his great-grandfather Frank Emil Rother. One of the church windows features St. Aloysius, a gift of Friedrich Schmitt, his maternal great-grandfather. And Stanley must have known that his great-grandfather Schlect was the one who carved the artwork at the top of the pillars in the church. Perhaps he even found inspiration when he gazed at the window of St. Francis Xavier, the 16th-century Jesuit missionary to the Far East — a gift from two other missionaries, Bishop Meerschaert and his own pastor, Monsignor Steber.

We don't know exactly when, or for how long, Stanley discerned his priestly vocation. In truth, the long-standing assumption in the family, and for most of the boys in his graduation class, was that Stanley would become a farmer like his father, and his father's father.

We do know that Betty Mae announced her vocation decision first. She told her parents that she was ready to skip senior year and join the community of sisters that had been so present and active in her entire life, the Adorers of the Blood of Christ.

When Stanley finally told them his news, his parents were more than a little surprised by the announcement.

"I didn't know he was going to the seminary," remembered Sister Marita. "I thought he was going to farm. We all did. I found out about his plans when we were both arranging to leave the same year — which wasn't too smart of us," she added. In retrospect, it must have been particularly difficult on their mother to say good-bye to both of them that same year.

Tom distinctly remembered the summer he turned 13. "First, they drove Betty Mae to the convent in Wichita, then my parents turned around and picked up Stan's luggage and drove him to San Antonio — all on the same trip." On a practical level, "it was hard on us when they left. Sister Marita used to help me dig potatoes, and that was over. And Stan helped milk cows, so Jim and I had to take care of the cow milking and all the chores. Then my dad always had a hundred acres of alfalfa to put up, so that put the load on us, and the plowing and the combining."

Indeed, life would never be the same for the Rother family after that year.

Everything Changes: The First Seminary

In September 1953, 18-year-old Stanley began the first of two years at St. John's Seminary, a preparatory program in San Antonio, Texas, designed for young men arriving straight out of high school.

Even for a disciplined farming teenager used to hard work, like Stanley, the rigorous and formulaic schedule of the school must have been a surprise. Rising bell at 5:30 a.m. Lights out at 10 p.m. Assigned times for prayer, meditation, and spiritual reading. Mass. Study and reading periods. Appointed recreation and relaxation hours.

Vincentian priests administered St. John's Seminary, and its sequel in graduate work, Assumption Seminary. A religious community that pioneered higher education throughout the Midwest and Texas in the early 1900s, the Vincentians had a special charism for missions and seminary education.

As Father Monahan noted, "[T]hey pushed what they considered sound piety, an adequate understanding of holy things, adherence to the rules of the house and the essentials of being a gentleman."[6]

St. John's seminary was located next to Nuestra Señora de la Purísima Concepción de Acuña, one of San Antonio's five mission churches founded by Spanish Franciscans in the early 1700s. From its architectural design to its artistic frescoes and limestone carvings, the historic mission church must have fascinated and surprised Stanley as he attended daily Mass there with the other seminarians — a foreshadowing of an even older Spanish church he would encounter years later.

Stanley completed the first year at St. John's without incident, and he went home to Okarche the following summer to work the family farm, helping his father and brothers with the harvest.

During those early seminary years, "Stan would always be home for harvest," recalled Tom. "Dad would run one combine and Stan would run the other one." One particularly busy harvest, "Dad and Jim were cutting wheat with one combine and Stan and Father Von Elm were binding oats at the same time," Tom remembered. Father Von Elm not only visited the Rother farm with great frequency, but one summer he also made money for his vacation by working by the hour for Franz Rother.

One of Stanley's close seminary friends, Joseph Hybner, remembered enlisting his help in planting holly bushes and American elm trees on the campus, many of which are still standing. "Stanley was very strong, very tough. If we needed something moved, we called on Stanley." Joe, who was also from a farming family, explained, "We weren't afraid of work."

During one school break, Stanley and a group of seminarians traveled with Joe to his hometown of Shiner, Texas, where they visited the Shiner Brewery and danced at a community dance hall. The next day, the two young men visited the local Catholic high school and were taken by surprise when some of the girls in the school recognized them: "Those are the guys we danced with last night!"

Stanley's courses in his first two years at St. John Prep were pretty basic: speech, logic, English, education, religion, and Latin. And his grades were mediocre, at best, including an A in religion, but Ds in English and logic.

Decades later, Sister Marita was surprised to find out that Stanley began keeping a daily diary during his second year at St. John's. His entries were succinct and almost always factual, listing events he attended and people he was with. But perhaps not surprising, what never varied were his frequent remarks about the weather.

On September 6, 1954, the beginning of his second year at St. John's, he wrote: "Arrived at Seminary today. Saw the show 'The Egyptian.' Started our half-day recollection tonight after night prayers. Warm. Weight 168."

Stanley wrote his diary as though he was talking to some-one, although obviously not expecting that anyone else would read it. He often mentioned receiving or writing letters to family, in particular to home, meaning to his parents.

His journal entries also revealed an early and sincere concern about his studies, including his ability to succeed in the seminary. In spite of the limited four-line space allowed by his journal for each day's entry, it is significant how often Stanley mentioned how long he spent on classes, whether or not he was prepared for a class — even listing the grades he received.

In November 1954, for example, Stanley recorded in his journal the grades for his first quarter of studies:

Speech C	Religion A
Logic D–	Latin C–
English D–	
Education C–	

Looking over her brother's journal entries decades later, Sister Marita observed: "He was honest and open, baring his feelings in some regard, acknowledging he had faults, and open about his relationships with the priests and other seminarians, as well as his relationship with Mary, Mother of God, and his God."

It wasn't until reading the journals that Sister Marita learned that it was in his late teens, maybe 20, when Stanley developed the habit of smoking a pipe. Not surprising, said Sister Marita, is how important Mass, prayer, and the sacraments continued to be for him. Reading over the entries, she explained that "it is obvious to me that prayer was an important part of his day, mentioning saying the Rosary 'during Lent after dinner,' or 'after supper every day.' [Stanley also] noted at times about his daily meditation, sometimes how sleepy he was, and occasionally, how he thought he had a good meditation."

As his journal entries indicate, Stanley inserted his concerns over family situations into his regular prayer routines: such as saying the Rosary for one of the relatives or praying a novena for two uncles and an aunt who married into the family and were not Catholic. But Sister Marita also noticed how often he seemed to get sick or have health problems during those first years in the seminary, perhaps caused by the stress of the unfamiliar and demanding situation.

Toward the end of his second year, Stanley wrote, "Am thinking about another vocation." But his director, he later added, "set me straight on another vocation and asked me to get my eyes checked," which he did. Hoping that glasses would improve not only his eyesight but also his ability to understand what was on the chalkboard, Stanley got glasses, even though he seems to have never made a regular practice of wearing them.

Glasses or no glasses, Stanley had a dreadful third year in the seminary. His seminary group of students had now progressed to Assumption Seminary for the next stage of their studies. Stanley's third year in the seminary was supposed to be a two-year course in philosophy, known as Philosophy I and Philosophy

II. This was followed by four years in theology. At the time that Stanley attended the seminary, the classes were taught in English, but all the main textbooks were in Latin. "Stan always found philosophy difficult," remembered one of his classmates, adding that it didn't help matters that the philosophy textbooks were in Latin. In 1956, at the end of his third year, the faculty informed 21-year-old Stanley that his grades were so poor that he had to repeat the academic year of Philosophy I.

Where Do You Find God?

If Stanley had been asked directly a theological question such as "Where is God?" it is fairly certain that he would have answered, "I find God in serving people, and in the work of my hands." As it was, Stanley responded to this statement of faith not with his words, but with his actions.

While he struggled academically to stay afloat, Stanley was at the same time working in many activities, especially outdoor or manual work. He worked in the seminary's bindery, almost daily. He spent four days building a shrine to the Blessed Virgin on campus. He leveled dirt on the front lawn, cleaned rooms, printed cards, repaired equipment, and picked pecans. If it needed doing, he did it. If it was broken, he fixed it. Looking back at Stanley's actions during those years, his fellow seminarians noted, "His work was a way of meditation" and "I have a feeling, when he was riding on that mower he spent a lot of time praying."

During the spring semester that he turned 22 years old, Stanley continued his battle to keep up with classes. His journal entries recorded small victories — "Gave sermon this morning" and "Had nice Latin class" — as well as disappointments with himself when he failed to fulfill his duties: "Late again for Mass." It is also worth mentioning that he recorded, almost as if keeping a mental daily list of successes, the manual work he was able to accomplish: "Did dishes duty," "Fixed laundry after lunch," "Worked in bindery 2½ hrs.," "Cleaned up auditorium," "Drained water in Barrmobile and tractor," "Raked leaves." In a persistently frustrating academic setting, it's not difficult to understand Stanley's need to get something "right" by doing service work and helping others. Those journal entries often concluded in words similar to the ones for November 30, 1957: "Tired and happy."

Stanley "was always working around the yard and fixing things," remarked his fellow seminarian and close friend Father Armando Escobedo, a native of the Texas Rio Grande Valley. "It was very rare during 'recreation time' that he would take recreation!" In his trademark generosity of service, Stanley bound a Bible in the seminary bindery for Armando as a gift, and years later sent him a stole from Guatemala.

"Stan and I were farm boys," noted Father Escobedo. "Maybe our difficulties brought us together. He made up for his scholastic problems in many other ways ... he made up for that in his kindness. His arms were always open to other people." Armando remembered telling Stanley that the seminary was taking advantage of him and his "free labor." But Stanley answered back, "Oh, no. Don't worry about it."

When Armando Escobedo was ordained on June 6, 1964, Stanley showed up at the cathedral in Corpus Christi, saying simply, "Did you think I was going to miss this?" The two friends stayed in touch over the years through letters and phone calls. On one of his drives south to Guatemala, Stanley and Father Sam Leven spent two nights visiting with Father Escobedo at his parish. That was probably the last time the two friends saw each other in person.

In addition to manual labor, Stanley's other outlet for enjoyment and relaxation was music. At Assumption Seminary, he was a member of the choir, the Schola Cantorum. He also took piano lessons, noting in his journal the times he was able to set aside an opportunity to practice.

"The Okies at Assumption were very close. It was us against the Texans," joked fellow classmate Father James Stafford, explaining that Oklahomans were the largest single diocesan group attending Assumption Seminary in those days, not counting the Archdiocese of San Antonio. Father Stafford remembered Stanley as "very reliable, very steady, very consistent, with his feet on the ground. He was a genuinely good person. I have a rosary that Stan repaired for me." Stanley was even the seminarian's barber, added Father Stafford — for the payment of 50 cents, a rate set "by fiat of the seminary authorities."

Although Stanley repeated Philosophy I successfully, things continued to get more difficult the following year. In the academic year 1957-58, Stanley barely passed the second year in philosophy. The course work had become more demanding, and his falling grades reflected his academic struggle. At this point in the seminary program, there were no classes like "Music" or "Religion," which Stanley usually did well enough in to bring up his grade-point average. Nevertheless, although he was asked to retake several exams, he was not forced to repeat the academic year of Philosophy II.

Then came the academic disaster that was his first year of theology. After five and a half years, nothing could save his inadequate grades and his inability to conquer the textbooks in Latin.

In 1959, five days into the second semester of Theology I, Stanley was told he had failed the fall semester — and the 23-year-old was sent home. The seminary rector told Stanley that the faculty, as a group, had decided that he could no longer continue at Assumption Seminary. In his journal entry, Stanley succinctly noted, "*Voluntas Dei* ['the will of God']. It's hard but no emotions yet."

In retrospect, his Oklahoma classmate Father James Stafford and some of his other classmates remarked in their interviews that the Vincentians took advantage of Stanley, his skills, and his willingness to do manual work. They described him as "innocent, not overly pious, but a good example of a man of prayer."

Decades later, when interviewed about him, Father Thomas Kavanaugh, one of Stanley's professors at Assumption, recalled, "Stanley was probably one of the finest students we ever had, but he had a devil of a time with the books." Father Kavanaugh then added, "His hardship with the books did not in any way sour him. He had a sense of his own dignity and his own worth when he had a chance to do something. Stanley was always neat and clean, a model in every way ... a peaceful individual."

Interestingly enough, although he failed his academic studies at Assumption, the seminary still claimed Stanley as part of its distinguished history. In published public records by the Texas State Historical Association regarding the seminary's history, the archives documented: When Assumption-St. John's concluded 75 years of service to higher education in Texas in 1990, "it has produced *one martyr*, ten bishops, and about 650 priests from its staff and alumni."

When Stanley's fifth-grade teacher, Sister Clarissa Tenbrink, heard the news that he had flunked out of seminary, she wrote Stanley a letter to encourage him. "He wanted to be a priest so badly. He was very discouraged. So I reminded him of the Curé of Ars," making a reference to French priest St. Jean-Baptiste-Marie Vianney. Much like Stanley, Father Vianney struggled in his academic studies and was notably deficient in Latin. He is now the patron saint of all priests.

"I told Stanley that if he really wanted to be a priest," Sister Clarissa said, then he should "pray, and trust, and God would take care of things."

CHAPTER 3

A New Beginning

The day that Stanley left San Antonio, the rector of Assumption Seminary wrote a letter to Oklahoma City's Bishop Victor Reed: "I deeply regret to inform you that we have had to ask Mr. Stanley Rother to discontinue his studies for the priesthood. This young man has continually had difficulty in his class work and at the end of this present half year we find he has failed in his moral theology and his dogmatic theology. Consequently, since he has already repeated one year in his course, we feel that it is unjust to him and to the diocese to allow him to continue. Therefore, we have advised him to leave and he seemed quite aware of the fact that he lacks intellectual ability to continue on for the priesthood."

When Stanley and his hastily packed bags got off the plane at Oklahoma City's Will Rogers Airport, Franz and Gertrude Rother were at the gate waiting for him. As parents, they must have felt a mixture of relief at being able to see him in person after hearing the shocking news, to hug him, and to reassure him as best they could — along with genuine concern for the well-being of their oldest son, and his future.

It was Stanley's pastor, Father Edmund Von Elm, who drove him to a dinner that night with Monsignor S. F. Luecke, the diocesan director of vocations. And it was the three men together who proceeded to Bishop Victor Reed's house for the unexpected meeting that would discuss Stanley's situation.

There is no official or written record of that meeting, only Stanley's concise mention in his journal: "Saw Bishop and he will send me on next fall."

Yet that one sentence is enough to assume that a very personal, candid, and open discussion must have taken place. With less than a year under his belt as bishop of Oklahoma, Bishop Reed did not know Stanley very well. But something must have happened during that fateful meeting that made Bishop Reed confident enough about Stanley and his desire to study for the priesthood to trust that a new seminary would be found for him.

When Stanley's sister heard about his failure in San Antonio, she was very disappointed. "I didn't know how to deal with it. I was alone in Wichita and was deeply sad that it had happened," Sister Marita remembered. "But I kept praying that if that's what he was supposed to do, that there would be a way for him to do it."

She also had a difficult time understanding what happened to Stanley to make him fail academically. "I am of the firm belief that he didn't learn the material because other things appealed to him. The farmer was still in him, so if he had an opportunity to go out and plant things, he did it! He neglected what he didn't want to do, and that was to learn a language," Sister Marita said, regarding Stanley's struggle with the Latin textbooks. "I don't think I really hold that as an excuse for him, but I do see that as my remembrance of him. Because I know that my parents were very strict with us, and doing our best was a very important value in our family."

After what must have been a difficult month of introspection at home in Okarche, the diocese asked Stanley to move to the new and as yet unopened St. Francis de Sales Seminary in northwest Oklahoma City. Stanley was not asked to attend the minor seminary, but instead to help work on and prepare the building for use. Because of this unusual assignment, Stanley Rother holds the distinction of being the first person to sleep overnight in the structure that currently serves as a conference center, pastoral center, and a retired priests' complex for the Archdiocese of Oklahoma City.

Stanley spent the next three months preparing the large building that would serve the statewide diocese as the preparatory seminary for young men in high school and the first two years of college. He repaired. He painted. He cleaned. He installed. He landscaped the grounds. In retrospect, it seems likely that the amount and the type of work that Stanley was engaged in full-time was probably the best possible healing and recovery for his wounded confidence.

What he didn't know, noted Father Monahan in his unpublished biography, was the difficulty that vocations director Monsignor Luecke was having in locating a suitable seminary for him. "A student for the priesthood with his scholastic record did not beget enthusiasm for acceptance on the part of seminary rectors."

According to Father Monahan, one of the seminaries that Monsignor Luecke contacted replied with a candid letter that stated: "We cannot accept this student for the reason that we have at present such a proportion of seminarians in our charge who are below average in intellectual ability that we are compelled to turn down, at least for a few years, any further applications for such students."[7]

In June 1959, the diocese sent Stanley to enroll in a summer course at Conception Seminary in northwest Missouri, an apostolate of the Benedictine monks of Conception Abbey. He enrolled in two summer classes: a special section of Latin and a class on Catholic worship. Meant specially as a concentrated language experience to improve his Latin — and his confidence — it instead seemed to develop further disappointment and frustration for him. "Took final (midterm) test in Latin 13 and probably failed," he wrote in his journal that summer. "Got grades today and I got a D in both courses.... Only one to get F for Saturday test.... Flunked vocab test today....Asked to recite in class but didn't have sentence translated.... Got test back in hymns and flunked again."

The rapidly crumbling circumstances depressed Stanley. "The promise of doing better at his next seminary, wherever it might be, was fading for him. He began walking in his sleep. He noted in the diary that his roommate told him he had walked across the roommate's bed twice in one night.... On Aug. 1, he wrote:'Didn't study much for afternoon test and I did badly. Am pretty disgusted and wish I could quit now.'Those are the words of a thoroughly discouraged, disheartened young man."[8]

Yet by the end of the summer, Stanley's resolve to continue God's plan for him as a path to the priesthood had returned.

In an August letter to Monsignor Luecke, his vocation director, Stanley wrote:

There is so much to learn in this short time, but this school can't be beat for good teachers and methods. My grades are not the best, but that doesn't mean that I didn't learn much this summer.... I don't know if I didn't get your letter or that you are having a hard time

finding a place for me, but I am anxious to know where
I will go for Theology in the fall. There is still time left
but I don't want to be left out when school starts.

Stanley also suggested in his letter that perhaps his place was
at St. Gregory's, the local Catholic college in Shawnee, Oklahoma, run by the Benedictine brothers and priests.

A week later Stanley received the reply: "You are to enter
first Theology at Mt. St. Mary's Seminary, Emmitsburg, Maryland. Opening date is September 11."

When she received news in September 1959 that Stanley
had left for Emmitsburg to repeat the first year of theology, Sister
Marita, who was teaching an overflowing class of 35 to 40 eighth-
graders in Wichita at the time, remembered enlisting her students'
assistance. "I got them involved in praying daily for Stanley ... a
few of them remember that even now, decades later, and they've
talked to me about how they participated in Stanley's journey."

Mount St. Mary's

In contrast to the big, long horizons and rolling farm country he was used to seeing in Okarche, at first sight, Mount St.
Mary's Seminary in Maryland must have seemed like a foreign
landscape to Stanley. Located near the base of Catoctin Mountain, on the easternmost ridge of the Blue Ridge Mountains, the
Mount Seminary and its adjoining college campus extend for
over 1,200 acres of stunning scenery.

The town of Emmitsburg itself is a seedbed of Catholic history dating back to its founding in 1785. That's 122 years before

Although he could follow the slower hesitant Spanish of the Tz'utujil more easily, Stanley never achieved complete command of the Spanish language. Yet it's a testament to his character and humility that he never stopped welcoming corrections when he tried speaking.

A year after completing the Spanish program, Stanley began to study the more intricate and complex Tz'utujil language, under the direction of Father Carlin. While continuing to participate in parish activities at Santiago Atitlán on weekends, Stanley began another intensive language-study immersion, spending Mondays through Fridays at the old Guatemalan capital of Antigua.

"This language is fantastic," Stanley wrote in a letter to Sister Marita. Explaining further, he wrote:

> It isn't related to any other besides the others here in Guatemala. There are 22 different Indian languages here. The Mayans reached the height of their civilization around the year 1,000 and had a very advanced culture. For some reason they declined and split up into groups or tribes when the Spanish came.... [T]hey were baptized in a wholesale manner, but they never gave up their culture and customs. They still haven't. They still have their language and especially in our area.

> It is highly structured and [there are] less exceptions than you find in other languages. The problem is just plain memory, how to say just what you want. Now I'm translating most thoughts from English to Spanish and then lingua [or Tz'utujil]. I can think somewhat

Oklahoma became a state. St. Elizabeth Ann Seton, the first U.S.-born saint, built her first Catholic girls' school in Emmitsburg, and her remains are entombed there. Above the town, high on the mountainside overlooking Mount St. Mary's and the National Shrine of St. Elizabeth Ann Seton, stands one of the oldest replicas of the Lourdes Grotto in the United States, built only two decades after Our Lady's apparition in 1858 at Lourdes, France. Mount St. Mary's is the oldest independent Catholic college in the United States — as well as the second-oldest Catholic college and the second-oldest Catholic seminary in the country.

Stanley and one of his uncles made the 1,300-mile trek from Okarche, Oklahoma, to Emmitsburg, Maryland, in a truck, arriving at Mount St. Mary's on September 10, 1959. He spent the next several days exploring the beautiful woods and mountains surrounding the historic setting. Everything about the place, from its history to its geography and extensive Catholic roots, demanded that Stanley take a fresh new look at the seminary. Not a bad site for a do-over.

In the words of Father Monahan, "Perhaps the greatest plus about Emmitsburg for Stanley was the rector, Msgr. George Mulcahy. He adopted a completely positive attitude about the new Oklahoman's prospects of academic success and eventual worth as a priest.... The gentlemanly, sometimes high-handed, monsignor brought to his role as rector the background of a working parish priest and a chancery office veteran. While he understood that a certain degree of learning was necessary to be a decent priest, he also knew that other characteristics — good judgment, stability, integrity, health, an active faith and prayer life, and zeal — were more important for a parish priest than an A in theology."[9]

At the end of Stanley's first semester at Mount St. Mary's Seminary, Monsignor Mulcahy reported to Oklahoma's Bishop Reed, "Mr. Rother's report is quite satisfactory. He has made an excellent impression thus far."

Perhaps it was because of the fresh new start. Or perhaps it was due to Stanley's maturing, and simply being older. But the fact remains that Stanley's journal entries during his years at the Mount carry a steady optimism that was not present during his years at St. John's and Assumption in San Antonio. His remarks about classes and study habits continued, but the tone was much lighter — "Finished Latin-Gk. N.T. for Lent." "Explained Moral exam to Fr. DePaw & he raised grade to 85."

This time around, Stanley recorded a lot more about activities, food, and outings than he did about manual work — and his typical two-word entries often became longer: "Left for Washington after breakfast & went to John McGiverni home for breakfast & dinner. Saw Franciscan Monastery, Immaculate Conception Shrine & Catholic University."

Even his farmer attentiveness to the weather returned: "Raining all morn." "Freezing this morning." "Misty all day." "55° now." "Foggy tonite & 30° may snow." "Rains came," followed by "Still raining now" in the same entry. "News tonight said Okla. had low temperatures and approx. 6" of snow." But the area that remained the same were his entries regarding his personal prayer or seminary prayer practices, noting feast days and celebrations: "Sol. High Mass of Blessed Virgin Mary." "Went to Grotto & lit 154 candles." "Confession." "Exposition & Holy Hour at 6:00." "Took care of candles at Grotto & lit 64."

At the Mount, as he had at Assumption, Stanley joined his well-regarded tenor voice to the seminary's Schola and participated in the school's dramatic productions. As his journal entries testified, he loved to take part in sports of all kinds — and at the Mount, he enjoyed taking long walks and treks in the mountains. Stanley established a bookbindery at the Mount, putting his skills and knowledge in this area to work for the various seminary classes, and even for the faculty.

Monsignor Hugh J. Phillips, the college librarian and director of the Grotto, remembered Stanley's frequent visits on his own to the Marian shrine: "He had a tender devotion to the Blessed Mother." When Stanley asked the monsignor for his prayers, the older priest assured him, "Stan, don't worry; love is going to pull you through."

Many of his classmates noted seeing Stanley frequently at the Grotto, remembering that he helped to make the Grotto's rock wall. "The seminarians would go there to rake leaves. Stan was there all the time," said his classmate Father William La Fratta of Virginia. "Stan was loved by everybody, a nice guy." He was a "mediocre student, but a real plugger."

The seminarians in that class had a special spirit, Father La Fratta remarked, and the group "looked out for one another." One way that the seminarians helped one another out was by translating from Latin into English the textbooks for the principal courses, like Dogmatic and Moral Theology.

Much like his classmates in San Antonio, Stanley's classmates at the Mount frequently noted the Oklahoman's desire to be of service. "As quiet as he was, he always had something bright about him," recalled Monsignor Joseph Kohut, who was ordained for the Diocese of Bridgeport, Connecticut. Stanley loved serving people, he said, adding, "A beautiful guy."

Of the 20-some members of his seminary class at Emmitsburg, 22 would be ordained priests. Twenty members of
the class were connected to dioceses located in the eastern
half of the country, one from Puerto Rico. Stanley was the
only Westerner, and most likely the only one from a farming
background.

In between seminary years, Stanley continued going home
to Okarche and helping with farm duties and harvesting with
his father Franz and his brothers, Tom and Jim. In his journal
entry for August 13, 1960, Stanley described a typical day at
the Okarche farm: "6:30 Mass & Comm[union]. Finished baling
a few bales in SW field. Dad one-wayed weeds in both fields
along the creek. Hauled in bale over south & loaded 2 loads
from SW. John W. got 340 bales for $17.50. Father out again
tonite. Washed hair."

During 1963, his final year at the Mount, Stanley's grades
were remarkably solid:

Dogma 76	Liturgy 87	
Moral Theology 82	Homiletics 85	
Scripture 88	Chant 92	
Canon Law 80	Past. Med. 79	Past Pract. 90

Father Thomas Connery, a classmate from the Diocese of
Albany, has maintained a special appreciation for Stanley's gifts
and his contribution to the class. Father Connery remembered
spending some of their free time hiking the mountains, and
going to the Grotto with Stanley to "prepare the place, working together. Stan had a great love and devotion for the Virgin
Mary," and the Grotto was a special place of prayer for him. In

his second year at the Mount, Stanley was named assistant Grotto chairman, becoming Grotto chairman the following year.

Ordained on the same day for different dioceses, both friends went on to serve the Church in mission territory, although in opposite directions — Father Connery for 10 years in Alaska and, of course, Father Stanley for 13 years in Guatemala. He remembers Stanley's "gentle spirit and easy way about him. He was a big, strong, generous man. He was easy to meet, and easy to get along with, an open spirit." Stanley influenced their small, close-knit class with his "discipline and prayerful spirituality."

One of their classmates who was later the rector of Mount St. Mary's Seminary, Archbishop Harry Flynn of the Archdiocese of St. Paul and Minneapolis, remembered Stanley's "life of recollected spirit" and the "prayerful presence he had before the Lord.... I was envious of the real gift of prayer that Stanley had ... he was in touch with God immediately when he entered the chapel."

During Stanley's final year at the Mount, he met regularly with a "Mr. Hall" at the tuberculosis sanatorium, sharing his faith experience and teaching him Catholic doctrine. On May 9, 1963, Stanley baptized Mr. Hall — most likely Stanley's first baptism.

A couple of weeks later, on May 21, 1963, Stanley left Emmitsburg, having successfully completed seminary studies at Mount St. Mary's.

Historian Father Monahan recorded the official memorandum written by the Mount's rector, Monsignor George Mulcahy:

> Mr. Rother spent four years at Mount St. Mary's after having difficulties at a former seminary because of studies.

He has given satisfaction here in every way, although he was cautioned several times not to let extra-curricular work interfere with his studies. This was his difficulty at the former seminary.

Mr. Rother's parents are farmers and he was raised on a farm. Mr. Rother is an expert with tools and in all manual arts. He is a man of good common sense and practical judgment. He is not afraid of work and is very generous in giving himself to worthy causes.

Mr. Rother's mother and father are devout Catholics. A sister is a Sister Adorer of the [Blood of Christ]. He has two unmarried brothers at home.

This young man was well received here by his brother seminarians and entered fully into the life of the community. He capably fulfilled several extra-curricular duties and showed initiative by inaugurating some new activities. He exhibits a manly piety. He is able to preach satisfactorily, showing a talent for simple instruction.

With God's grace, he should be a very effective and valuable parish priest.[10]

Ordination Day: May 25, 1963

On May 25, 1963, Francis Stanley Rother was ordained a priest forever by Bishop Victor Reed at the Cathedral of Our Lady of Perpetual Help in Oklahoma City. He was one of 11 priests ordained that day for service in the Diocese of Oklahoma City and Tulsa. Ironically, by 1970, a mere seven years later, five of the 11 had left the priesthood. Those five had been considered the "best and brightest" of their class.

"Ordination was a very joyous time, and our whole family was there to celebrate it," said Sister Marita. She knew it meant a lot to Stanley because he "had a lot of love for his family and his extended family," recalling that she still had a beautiful case that Stanley made in the bookbindery for her breviary and brought it back as a gift for her from the Mount. "We didn't have a lot of time then because I had to get back to school. I was working on my master's at that time. But what stands out in my memory is that Stanley seemed so much at peace and very content."

At a priestly ordination, each candidate is called by name. Each one, literally, answers that summons. Biographer Father Monahan described the ritual, drama, and ceremony of the occasion:

> "*Franciscus Stanislaus Rother*," the bishop's assistant called loudly. Stanley responded with a firm "*Adsum*" (I am here). The candidates lay face down on the floor as the chanted Litany of the Saints poured over them repeatedly asking the champions of Christ to pray for those being ordained.

> Then Bishop Victor Reed prayed over the 11, begging the Holy Spirit to rush upon them. In silence, he laid his hands on their heads one-by-one in a rite which goes back to the roots of the faith community in Jerusalem.

Later in the ceremony, Stanley's hands were smeared with fragrant chrism in a special rite to consecrate those hands for their holy work: celebration of the Eucharist, baptism, anointing of the sick, blessings. He knelt before the bishop, placed his hands in the bishop's hands, and solemnly promised obedience and respect to Bishop Reed and his successors.

Finally, the newly ordained priests vested with the traditional priestly liturgical garments, and celebrated the Eucharist with the bishop.

Immediately following the ordination Mass, the new priests gave individual blessings to their parents, other family members, friends, and other priests. One can imagine the proud joy with which Gertrude Smith Rother and Franz Rother knelt before their oldest child to receive his blessing. They were followed by Sister Marita, Jim [and Mary Lou], Tom, and many other Rothers.

In his diary, Stanley summed up the day with: "Very excited." For the reticent Father Stanley Rother that emotional state translates into something like extreme delight or overwhelming happiness.[11]

On one of Stanley's holy cards for his ordination, there is a prayer outlined:

Make him, O Lord, a priest according to Your Heart: meek, humble, zealous, so that all he does will be for

Your honor and glory. Mold him into a man of labor
and of prayer, insensible to earthly things, and sensible
only to Your Love and to the graces of the Holy Spirit.

Below it is a famous quote from St. Augustine, one that was
quoted widely following Stanley's bloody death: "For my own
sake I am a Christian; for the sake of others I am a Priest."

The following day, Father Stanley Rother was the celebrant
at a Solemn High Mass in his home parish of Holy Trinity in
Okarche.

"His first Mass in Okarche and reception was perfect," remembered his classmate and grade-school best friend from Holy
Trinity, Ralph Wittrock. "The sermon was wonderful, very organized and flowed just the way it was supposed to.... You've got
to admire Stan for his dedication. He was orderly within himself
... his goals were set higher."

It is not surprising that the church overflowed with people
— family, friends, and Holy Trinity classmates. The dinner that
followed was shared by 350 people, some of whom returned to
the church later in the day for Benediction of the Blessed Sac-
rament and a parish reception in honor of Father Stanley. That
night he wrote five words in his journal: "Took gifts home. Very
tired."

Ministry: The Early Years

There is no way to overstate the radical changes taking place in
the Catholic Church and American society during the 1960s,
when Father Rother began his priestly ministry.

Pope John XXIII had begun the massive undertaking of an ecumenical council to consider ways to renew the Church in the modern world, consider reforms, and promote unity in diversity within the universal Body of the Church. He convened the Second Vatican Council — known as Vatican II, on October 11, 1962 — summarized in his famous remark, "I want to throw open the windows of the Church."

Nine days after Stanley's ordination, Pope John XXIII died (June 3, 1963) — and within three weeks, Giovanni Battista Montini was elected pope, taking the name of Paul VI. He promptly announced his intent to continue with the council convened by his predecessor.

On the national scene, civil-rights demonstrations culminated in the arrest of Martin Luther King, Jr. On August 28, 1963, 250,000 people marched for civil rights in Washington, D.C. — the largest demonstration ever seen in the nation's capital, and one of the first to have extensive television coverage. On November 22, President John F. Kennedy was assassinated in Dallas, and Lyndon B. Johnson was sworn in as president of the United States.

"The 1960s was a decade of mass politics and mass marketing on a scale without precedent," wrote journalist Daniel Henninger. "It never stopped — demonstrations, assassinations, urban terrorists, and the drugs, movies, music and fashion that celebrated (and sold) all of it…. As relevant, the U.S. Supreme Court in the early '60s said simple prayers in public schools had to stop." In Oklahoma, 1963 marked the beginning of NAACP Youth Council sit-ins at lunch counters in Oklahoma City, and the founding of Oral Roberts University in Tulsa.

Even in rural Oklahoma, it would have been impossible for Father Stanley Rother to not be aware of and in some form influenced by the massive changes taking place in the world and in the Catholic Church.

But in the meantime, there was a harvest to take care of. Following his ordination, and while he waited to find out about his first pastoral assignment, it is not surprising that Stanley returned to the Rother farm to work with his father Franz, and his brothers Jim and Tom. By the end of the month, however, Father Stanley received the official call from the chancery informing him that he had been appointed assistant pastor of St. William Church in Durant, a small town in southeast Oklahoma.

While fellow members of his ordination class may have taken note of Stanley's less-than-average academic performance at the seminary — and of his rather unimportant ministry appointment, Stanley's first assignment took advantage of his unique strengths.

The Texoma Undertaking

The Diocese of Oklahoma City and Tulsa had recently acquired a tract of 95 acres of land on Lake Texoma, a large reservoir created by the U.S. Corps of Engineers by damming the Red River that divides the states of Texas and Oklahoma. Durant is conveniently located on the east side of the enormous lake. According to the rules put together by the Corps of Engineers, the Catholic Church, as a non-profit, would have use of this land over a long period of time for an exceptionally small fee — provided it improved the site. Naturally, Bishop Reed thought of Stanley and his practical knowledge of construction and mechanics.

That summer, Stanley and Bishop Reed toured the property on the lake and discussed plans. For the most part, the land was in its original tangled, forested state. Stanley was assigned the task of clearing the land and building cabins for a diocesan retreat. Stanley returned to the property to survey the situation with Father Joe Howell from Durant. "It was a dense tangle of briars," Father Howell described years later. "It was really something. What a mess that thing was down there. He never bragged, but he did a tremendous job."

According to Father Howell, "The bishop told me he was not to have any assignments except Masses" so that his time could be devoted to working at the Lake Texoma property. In reality, the division of tasks and work required was a bit more complicated. For starters, the Durant parish had three mission churches in three different counties under its care, which meant that on Sundays the two priests divided the duties and celebrated three Masses each. As is typical in spread-out rural areas, the whole circuit encompassing the missions was 83 miles long, a substantial effort.

Meanwhile, Stanley continued to spend any "free time" he could with his family in Okarche. On May 1, 1965, Stanley's youngest brother, Tom, married Martha Jane "Marti" Liebl at Holy Trinity Catholic Church in Okarche — and Stanley celebrated the Mass. Tom and Marti still live in the house where Franz and Gertrude raised Stanley and his siblings — and like them, they farm the land of their ancestors. During Stanley's first five years of ministry served in Oklahoma, he baptized Tom and Marti's first two children, Patrick, born in 1966, and Douglas, born in 1967. But their next three children were born while Stanley was in Guatemala.

In those large Rother family gatherings, Marti remembered best how Stanley played and talked with the kids: "He'd just go over to the little ones and pick them up and play with them … and they would be all over him." After he left for Guatemala, Stanley would always remember to bring his nephews and nieces something special on his visits, Marti noted, "whether a little shirt or poncho or a little bag … he'd always bring them something from Guatemala." When their oldest son graduated from eighth grade, Stanley made sure he was there to celebrate the Mass, and he brought his nephew a rosary, which Marti said Patrick still has.

Although Stanley remained in Durant only two years, the central focus of his work from 1963 to 1968 continued to be "doing something" with the diocesan property on Lake Texoma. In August 1965, Stanley was appointed associate pastor at St. Francis Xavier Church in Tulsa. A year later the bishop moved him to Holy Family Cathedral in Tulsa, but that assignment lasted only three months. And in September 1966, Stanley was named associate pastor at Corpus Christi parish in Oklahoma City.

Throughout all these transfers, Stanley's work at Lake Texoma continued. He spent weekends at the assigned parish and Monday to Friday at the lake site. Depending on the appointment, this meant he was regularly traveling considerable distances: From Tulsa to the lake site, 190 miles; and from Oklahoma City to the site, 140 miles.

Not all priests admired Stanley's unique assignment at Lake Texoma, openly judging Stanley's physical work on the buildings and landscaping. Stanley confessed to his friend Father Don Moore that he knew some priests "were making fun of me, saying to me, 'What are you doing at Lake Texoma? That's not priests' work.' " Stanley was aware of at least one senior priest whom he admired who had remarked, "We may have made a mistake in ordaining Stan Rother." According to Father Moore, that statement "cut Stan very deeply ... he was a very private man." Yet Stanley also confided to Father Moore that Bishop Reed, responding to criticisms regarding his use of Stanley's talents, said, "Stan Rother is one of the few priests I can trust to work hard out of my sight."

Indeed, with no master plan, no set budget, and no available outside resources for Stanley to reach out to for help, the Texoma project is hard to describe — and certainly, one of a kind. Stanley looked for assistance wherever he could. High school boys from Durant worked as volunteers. Stanley's father Franz drove from the farm when he could, to lend a hand. Marshall County provided him with some of the equipment. And his friend Father Moore became a frequent volunteer.

The Texoma project reached its climax of intensity from March to October 1966, with Stanley working at the site nearly full time. During that period, he apparently lived at the lake, according to his own written summary of his assignments as a priest. "I imagine that was a spiritual time for him," surmised Father James Stafford.

Looking back on that intense physical experience makes Texoma and those years when Stanley spent so much time alone seem like a desert experience, a time of physical, mental, and spiritual preparation for his next ministry — the vocation of his life. And although we have no way of knowing exactly what he was thinking, like so much that is true about Stanley Rother's life, he spoke with his actions.

When he was finished, Stanley had successfully constructed four buildings by creatively modifying seven World War II prefabricated units formerly located at the University of Oklahoma in Norman. The largest of the four dwellings consisted of three prefabs ingeniously joined to include a large entryway, a living room, a kitchen, seven bedrooms, and two baths. The two smaller buildings each contained a living room, a kitchen, and a bath. One of them, meant to be the bishop's cabin, had one bedroom. The other unit had two bedrooms. There was also a caretaker's house at the entrance of the property, similarly made by two combined prefabs.

The property and its buildings are still in use by the Archdiocese of Oklahoma City.

Stanley's First Work with Indians

Growing up in Oklahoma, whose very name is Choctaw for "Land of the Red Man," Stanley Rother was conscious of American Indians and their various tribal designations.

But it was during his two years in Durant that Stanley developed exceptional, lasting friendships with members of American Indian tribes. The family he grew closest to in Durant was that of Gordon and Selah Schulze, both converts to the Catholic Church. Gordon was an Oklahoma Highway Patrol trooper who, on occasion, allowed Stanley to ride with him in his patrol cruiser to give them a chance to talk. Selah Rose (Lewis) was half Creek and part Choctaw, and she grew to consider Stanley as part of their family. "He ate with us. He counseled us. He was one of the best friends we ever had," Selah said. "He was well

liked in Durant, so kind and so good." The Schulzes' three children also got to know Stanley well. Their oldest son, Gordon Jr.,
was an altar server for him at St. William's and became a helpful
volunteer for Stanley when clearing the land at Lake Texoma.

One day during that first semester, a freshman named Carol
met Stanley on the campus of Southeastern State College, in
Durant, now Southeastern Oklahoma State University. Father
Stanley was dressed in casual clothes, and one of her friends
whispered to Carol, "He's a priest." Carol was nearly 100 percent
American Indian — a mixture of the Caddo, Cheyenne, Chero-
kee, and Seneca tribes. She was raised in a Protestant church
and had been led to believe that Catholics were idol worshipers.
Yet she was attracted to the Catholic Church. So when a friend
invited her to Mass at St. William's Church, she met once again
the young priest she had seen at the university.

The next time Carol saw Stanley on campus, she introduced
herself to him. "His eyes looked straight at you, the most beautiful
eyes," she remembered. Soon after that, Carol and a friend began
to visit Stanley at the parish regularly. "He knew how to make you
comfortable, how to make you talk. The conversations ranged from
religion to poltergeists to keeping a journal of one's life." It wasn't
long before Carol committed to studying Catholic doctrine.

When Carol's mother learned about her visits with a priest,
she was upset. But according to Carol, she came around to say,
"If you're going to become a Catholic, be the best Catholic you
can be."

That March, Carol left Durant because she was having serious issues with her boyfriend, whom Stanley had warned her
about. When she learned that she was pregnant, a doctor re-
ferred her to Catholic Charities in Oklahoma City, and Catholic

Charities placed her in the home of a reliable sponsor couple. "One day there was a knock on the door," Carol said. "I opened the door and [Stanley] was standing there. I burst into tears. He looked at me and said, 'We need to talk.' He really encouraged me. He told me he would be praying for me, and said, 'There's a plan for your life … you're part of a bigger plan. You just have to remember and to learn to stand and not run away.' "

Eleven years later, when Carol entered the Catholic Church, there was a letter in her mailbox from Guatemala. "It's about time," Stanley wrote. The things he said to her, even when she was half listening, were "like seeds planted," Carol added. "To me he was like a shepherd."

An Oklahoma Mission in Guatemala

As early as 1960, Pope St. John XXIII asked the Churches of North America to lend pastoral assistance to the people of Central America, pleading: "It is necessary that all those who wish to share in the apostolic anxiety of Our heart, should make every effort and every sacrifice to meet the expectations of that great continent, Latin America."

A year later, Vatican diplomat Monsignor Agostino Casaroli took the papal plea even further by giving the pope's request for assistance a numerical goal. Speaking to the Conference of Major Superiors of Men and Women in the United States at the University of Notre Dame, Monsignor Casaroli pointed out the dire state of the Church in Latin America, urging that "this ideal is the following, that each religious province aim to contribute to Latin America in the next ten years a tithe — 10 percent — of its membership as of this current year."[12]

In the following decade, religious communities of men and women responded with great generosity, and so did dioceses throughout the United States.

"[The pope] asked the Catholics of the U.S. to send missionaries both lay and clerical to the assistance of their brethren in Latin America," Bishop Reed said in his homily at the 1963 commissioning Mass for Oklahoma's first foreign missionaries. "Now as a diocese, we formally accept the challenge of a Latin America Mission in a sister diocese named Sololá in Guatemala.... Christ is waiting for us, for you and me, in people — people in concrete situations — real people; the 'have nots,' specifically the Indians of Santiago Atitlán."

Bishop Reed presented crosses to four people who were leaving to serve the people of Guatemala, two priests and two laypersons — Father Ramon Carlin, Father Thomas Stafford, Dr. Joe Trimble (a Tulsa dentist), and his wife Kay. He noted that the undertaking was intended to be "an experiment in common brotherhood between our people of Oklahoma and the people of the parish of Santiago Atitlán in Guatemala."

Three others had committed themselves to three years of service and had already left Oklahoma for Santiago Atitlán: Father Robert O'Brien and two single laymen, Patrick Pyeatt and Jerry Arledge. A fifth layperson, Marcella Faudree, a veteran nurse, joined the original Oklahoma mission group later that fall.

The five laypeople from Oklahoma who volunteered for the Guatemala mission were part of the nearly 1,000 people from the United States who volunteered during the 1960s as part of the Papal Volunteers for Latin America (PAVLA) — an organization formed by Rome in 1960 for Catholic laypeople from any country who wanted to become missionaries in Latin America.

How the Diocese of Oklahoma City and Tulsa paired up with the newly formed Diocese of Sololá in Guatemala seems rather random, although it could also be called providential. When Bishop Reed sent Father Ramon Carlin to Guatemala, the diocesan priest looked at several locations, eventually meeting in person with Italian Franciscan missionary Bishop Angélico Melotto. Bishop Melotto had immigrated to Guatemala in 1950, after serving as a missionary priest for 14 years in China, before being expelled by its communist government.

Father Carlin found out that the Diocese of Sololá surrounded Lake Atitlán, a deep, dark blue lake enclosed by mountains and three towering volcanoes. The natural geographical beauty of the land stood in stark contrast to the terrible poverty of its overwhelmingly indigenous people, comprised of various communities, all descendants of the ancient Mayans.

"It will be a question not only of building up new economic structures among them," Bishop Reed expounded at the commissioning Mass that sent off Oklahoma's missionaries to Santiago Atitlán, "of improving their physical health, of new cooperative structures in trade and credit, but we must also reveal Christ to them. This, perhaps, will be the most difficult task because some of them may possess his Spirit in a greater degree than do we."

The bishop continued:

Somehow by going to the "have-nots" of the world, we will not only help them economically (and spiritually, we hope), but we will be helping ourselves even more.

The time is past, if indeed it was ever present, when the Church could stake out a mission in unknown territory and proceed to ignore the native genius of the people whom she evangelized. Today the Church wishes to listen as well as to speak. It is a lesson of history. She speaks the message of eternal salvation, but she is not deaf to the cries of social justice which break from the throats of the underprivileged of the world. The "have-nots" have aspirations put there by God and strengthened by a better human knowledge of the world, which inspire them to want to move to a level of life more in keeping with their dignity as persons. These aspirations are dynamite. Such people must be aided to realize their aspirations surely and peacefully on all fronts.

The Christian "renewal" of the people of Santiago Atitlán must come through a "dialogue" with them — the "have nots." There is much that we can learn from them. Christ hides himself in them and waits for us. We hope that our missionary work among them will result in a more resplendent revelation of Christ, both in them and in ourselves."

As a newly ordained priest, Stanley was ineligible to volunteer for Guatemala in 1963. But it would have been impossible for him not to be aware of his diocese's brand-new mission work. The Church in Oklahoma, a Catholic community that to this day remains a home mission diocese in the United States, would be sending missionaries to a village in Guatemala where the parish church building was constructed well before the Mayflower touched the shores of North America.

The Oklahoma team began to operate the mission at San-tiago Atitlán in the spring of 1964.

Why Me?

When Father Ramon Carlin invited Stanley out to lunch in spring 1968, the two of them had most likely never spent any considerable amount of time together. But as diocesan priests, they of course knew each other even in the most basic mode — and had probably heard stories about one another.

Among fellow Oklahomans, Ramon Carlin was known fondly as "Tex," a nickname that was likely given to him at the American College of the illustrious Catholic University of Lou-vain. Although born in Oklahoma, when Ramon Carlin first arrived in Belgium from San Antonio, he did so wearing a white Stetson hat, and the image stuck with him. Perhaps his nickname was also validated by Carlin's blunt, uncompromising style and his colorful personality.

A stout man of strong opinions, Father Carlin could make a person "spitting mad as easily as he could warm his heart," wrote former *Sooner Catholic* editor Jeanne Devlin, about the man in charge of the Oklahoma mission. "But it ran both ways. He was forever tracking down Catholics who had lost contact with the Church or fallen from favor.... He had strong opin-ions but didn't see himself as the only one with answers." As a young fortysomething priest when the mission was founded, he "fought hard for many of the liturgical changes that would be enacted by the Second Vatican Council. He never lost that fervor." And at the Guatemala mission, he insisted that its work be carried "by all believers — clergy, religious, and laity, and to his death, he lived what he preached."

By the time Bishop Reed named him the head of Oklahoma's Guatemalan mission project, Tex Carlin had already served the diocese as pastor in a handful of parishes, as a federal prison chaplain, as head of a Catholic high school, and as diocesan director of music, youth, and family life. He was a capable organizer, with an innate talent to inspire others to achieve shared goals.

There is no written record of the details of Ramon Carlin's lunch discussion with Stanley Rother. Yet we know the most important fact: Tex Carlin invited Stanley to join the mission team — and within hours, the same young man who once wrote in his journal "*voluntas Dei*," vowing to follow God's will in his life when his life and vocation seemed most uncertain, had said "Yes."

Oklahoma's Bishop Victor Reed appointed Father Stanley to the Guatemala mission team, effective mid-June 1968.

The original travel arrangements called for Father Stanley to fly to Guatemala with Bishop Reed. But when the bishop's schedule changed those plans, Father Stanley decided this was his opportunity to drive his own red-and-white Ford Bronco to the new assignment, all 2,000 miles of it.

In the fall of 1968, Stanley and veteran missionary Father Tom Stafford made the long trek together, and they did so with a 1,000-pound rock picker in tow. Whether driven by excitement, or simply impatient to get there, at one point the twosome alternated driving and kept going for 36 hours straight without resting. It still took them five days to get to Santiago Atitlán.

The deeper they drove into the western highlands of Guatemala, the rougher, bouncier, windier, and slower the drive became.

Looking out the window at the stunning landscape must have felt like watching a National Geographic documentary featuring one of the most beautiful places on earth.

Indescribable, stunning beauty. Mountains of deep, green foliage. Bright, vibrant colored flowers. And in the distance, the astonishing blue/green colors of the lake. Surrounded by mysterious, spectacular volcanoes wrapped in fast-moving clouds, the lake looks as if it had been colored by hand into a range of mountains.

The final 10-mile stretch between the villages of San Lucas Tolimán and Santiago Atitlán, normally taking 30 to 45 minutes by car, proved to be the most challenging. Halfway on a pothole-ridden road, Father Stanley heard and felt the ripping sound of the muffler being torn from the car.

As the two priests neared the town of Santiago, the number of people walking on the road increased, locals dressed in colorful indigenous clothes, most of them carrying heavy loads — the men carrying cargo on their backs, and the women carrying cargo on their heads.

Once they entered the town, Stanley and Father Stafford drove slowly on the narrow, winding streets, finally coming to a stop at the central open square — where they faced an impressive flight of steps that led up to the stately colonial church. They had finally arrived at MICATOKLA (the Misión Católica de Oklahoma, or Catholic Mission of Oklahoma) — the name that the first Oklahomans gave to the parish of Santiago, St. James the Apostle, reflecting its connection to the Diocese of Oklahoma

City and Tulsa. Stanley became the 12th member of the Oklahoma team, six of them priests.

When they finally parked the Bronco in front of the parish
church, Father Stafford turned to Stanley and unceremoniously
stated, "*Bienvenido a Santiago.*"

CHAPTER 4

MICATOKLA:
Stanley's New Home

A t five foot ten, Father Stanley would have stood out like a giant in a world of short indigenous people. And if his height did not make the good-looking Oklahoman stand out enough, his characteristic neatly trimmed, sandy-colored beard with a tinge of red did.

"The past two weeks have been revealing," 33-year-old Stanley wrote in his first letter to Sister Marita. "The people themselves are quite exceptional; there is great poverty ... the normal income for many families is $50 a year; their main staple is corn, grown on a little plot maybe as much as a three or four hour walk from their home."

Father Stanley went on to describe to Sister Marita the typical 12-by-12-foot thatched huts, with dirt floors, housing whole families — and the way that all the huts were crammed together in one-half square mile of the village where 15,000 Tz'utujil Indians lived.

The Tz'utujil people, indigenous Indians of Guatemala, are the fifth largest of the 21 Mayan ethnic groups that dwell in Guatemala.

The parish of Santiago Apóstol, which gives the town its name, is the oldest parish in the Diocese of Sololá. The Spanish

Franciscan friars founded it in 1536. The present church, considered a national monument by the Guatemala government, was built in 1541–1547, most probably on top of a Mayan temple site. In pre-Hispanic times, the town was the capital of the Mayan Tz'utujil nation.

In the 1870s, Guatemala had expelled all foreign priests, mostly Spaniards, and did not permit their return until the 1940s. So, ironically, when the first Oklahoma missionary group arrived at this 400-year-old parish, there had not been a resident priest at Santiago Atitlán for over a century. In terms of religion, the parish was as malnourished as its citizens were for food.

Santiago Atitlán and its neighboring villages were among the poorest places in Central America. Men earned 25 to 70 cents a day for agricultural labor, and more than half of all children died before the age of six. The most common causes of death were completely preventable: malnutrition, diarrhea, flu, and measles. Most adults had intestinal worms from drinking water directly from Lake Atitlán, the same source where they washed their clothes and bathed.

Four of the original six-member team who accompanied Father Ramon Carlin to Guatemala in 1964 were no longer there. But in 1965, Father Bob Westerman had come from Oklahoma, and two religious priests had joined the team by the time Stanley arrived in 1968: Jesuit anthropologist Father Jake Early and Father Jude Pansini, a Benedictine monk and an anthropologist-in-training.

Next to the church, a two-story rectory had been designed and built by the first group of Oklahomans on top of a partially completed rectory. The upstairs of the wing facing the church plaza included a large common room, complete with a fireplace in one corner — and a roofed second-story porch running the full length of the house.

In that first letter to Sister Marita, Father Stanley described what must have been the most alien of all natural features he'd ever encountered. "Several of us climbed a 11,200 foot volcano the other day," he wrote, "and we came to the last cornfield only after a three-hour climb." The town of Santiago Atitlán, in fact, is nestled where the slopes of three great volcanoes come together: Volcán San Pedro, across the inlet to the west, rising more than 10,000 feet; Volcán Tolimán, immediately behind the town and more than two miles above sea level; and Volcán Atitlán.

In his 1934 travel book *Beyond the Mexique Bay*, British writer Aldous Huxley compared the beauty of Lake Atitlán to Italy's Lake Como. The Italian body of water, he wrote, "touches the limit of the permissibly picturesque." Atitlán, however, "is Como with the additional embellishment of several immense volcanoes. It is really too much of a good thing." The lake takes its name from the fusion of simple Náhuatl words, with "Atit-lán," meaning simply "at the water." Its altitude of almost one mile above sea level provides for a mild, semi-tropical climate of mostly cool nights and pleasant days.

History runs deep in this part of the Americas and always intersects with its exceptionally volatile geology. Lake Atitlán, recognized as the deepest lake in Central America, occupies a portion of the Atitlán caldera — formed during an eruption of several cubic miles of lava about 84,000 years ago. It is located in an area between the coastal plains and the highlands in the southwestern part of Guatemala. Of the three volcanoes in or on the rim of the caldera, San Pedro is the oldest. It seems to have stopped erupting about 40,000 years ago. Tolimán began growing after San Pedro stopped erupting, and probably remains active. And Atitlán volcano has grown almost entirely in the last 10,000 years, and remains active, with its most recent eruption occurring in 1853.

Even to this day, no road circles the lake, which is located about 31 miles west-northwest of the ancient city of Antigua. The communities, towns and villages that surround Lake Atitlán are geographically and physically separated from one another, creating "isolated pockets of habitation.... Many of the villages may be separated from their neighbors by two miles or less, and yet being isolated ... they may have distinct economies, dress, and even vocabularies."[13] Indeed, the history of these lakeside communities is as complex, if not quite as ancient, as its volcanoes — distinct groups of people, each with their own traditions and languages, which in pre-Columbian times operated as rivaling nations of the ancient Maya civilization.

When the Oklahoma team arrived, over half of the people of Guatemala were indigenous, illiterate, and impoverished, most of Mayan descent, each speaking a different language, depending on their Mayan lineage. The more educated Ladinos, of Spanish or mixed Spanish/Indian descent, lived largely in the cities and controlled the bulk of the land, the wealth, and the power in the country.

MICATOKLA

By the time Stanley arrived in Santiago Atitlán in 1968, the Oklahoma mission group had initiated a flurry of programs —

many of which were already seeing concrete results after only four years.

Wanting to bring both Tz'utujil and Ladinos to greater participation in the Eucharistic liturgy, the team organized and trained parishioners to take part in singing and instrumental music, and to be adult altar servers, ushers, lay lectors, and extraordinary ministers of Holy Communion. They organized a more systematic religious education program, recruiting and training catechists for the instruction of children, young adults, and adults, especially those preparing for the sacraments of initiation and for marriage.

The team also founded a radio station, licensed in the name of the Tz'utujil, with a focus on literacy. Father Stafford did the technical side of setting up the radio station, and Sister Elizabeth Nick wrote the actual programming for the "Voice of Atitlán." Two lay volunteers, Penny Gerbich and Rita Weil, set up a Montessori school for the children.

One of the first service projects that the team established was a health clinic, where a number of nurse volunteers came to serve over the years, with a specialized nutrition center for malnourished children. After Father Stafford organized a farmers' cooperative, with its own commonly held land, other cooperatives followed, such as a weavers' co-op. A credit union was organized to do away with the criminal 10 percent a month interest rate of local lenders.

In addition to reconnecting the people to their longstanding Catholic faith and traditions, perhaps the most significant achievement of the Oklahoma mission team was Father Ramon Carlin's initiative in developing a written language for the

Tz'utujil. Although the Tz'utujil language extended back for innumerable centuries, it had no written tradition. The year before leaving for Guatemala, Father Carlin enrolled in an international linguistics course at the University of Oklahoma in Norman. And as soon at the team had settled in at Santiago Atitlán, he began the important work of learning the language in order to construct a written vocabulary.

As early as 1966, Father Carlin enlisted the help of two Tz'utujil men whom he discerned would be effective: Antonio Tzina Ratzan and Juan Mendoza. Antonio's background was as a merchant selling fruit, and Juan was a teenager working at the rectory. Father Carlin sent the two men to the Francisco Marroquín Language Institute in Antigua, where "they listened to how the sounds came out of our throats," Antonio recalled, and gradually formed a Tz'utujil alphabet. By the end of 1967, the three men had embarked on the tedious and intense work of building a Tz'utujil vocabulary and grammar. Working every day for eight hours a day, they sometimes invited groups as big as 15 to sit in on their sessions and lend their ears and voices to the painstaking process.

In Father Stanley's first year at Santiago Atitlán, on July 25, 1968, the town and the parish's feast day of St. James (Santiago), the people heard for the first time ever the translated prayers of the Mass and the readings for the day's liturgy in Tz'utujil.

Ironically, Father Carlin was never able to speak Tz'utujil well enough to carry on a conversation. As Antonio explained, "Padre Ramon couldn't change his voice. He had a gringo voice."

Fitting in at MICATOKLA

Stanley's first assignment at the mission was to repair the floor of a bathroom in the women's wing of the rectory complex. Since the downstairs area of the rectory was unfinished, Stanley transitioned into work he was very familiar with — cleaning, painting, installing light fixtures and electrical switches. This time, however, he had two Tz'utujil men assisting him, his first of many cooperative ventures with the local people.

Stanley was pleased to find himself as the 12th member of the MICATOKLA team. In addition to the six priests, the female side of the team included three Papal Volunteers — Marcella Faudree, Penny Gerbich, and Rita Weil — and three women religious — Ursuline Sisters Elizabeth Nick and Roberta Allen, and Maryknoll Sister Linda O'Brien.

In a very real way, learning to be a part of a large team of people serving the same parish must have been as strange and foreign for Stanley as the new unfamiliar culture he moved into. Everything about this team made Stanley out to be the alien one. He was used to hard work but not to team-style working. In Father Monahan's words, "Here he was a newcomer among veterans, a student with a shaky academic background in the midst of academic professionals and scholars, a self-contained young man caught in a household of numerous extroverts, a conservative Catholic at a time (the years immediately following the theological tremors of the Second Vatican Council) and a place (an extremely isolated rectory inhabited by a dozen church professionals thirsting for change) where the proposal of new concepts was the prevailing atmosphere, almost a sport."[14]

To make matters more difficult, Father Carlin's style of an "open rectory" meant that visitors to the rectory compound were not only welcome, they were encouraged. One visitor described the large downstairs at the rectory as a street where people could, and would, come in the front door any time, and leave out the back when they were ready. In the evenings, many Tz'utujil and Ladinos would be on the first floor playing board games — and being observed by Father Carlin or his staff. He had a theory that intellectually bright people could be identified by their competence at board games, which he supplied as a testing field.

"[Stanley] didn't really enter in at first," nurse Marcella Faudree recalled. "He knew he was the low man on the totem pole. He was a very kind person, not very outgoing. He pitched right in at the hospital." Sister Linda O'Brien explained the disconnection by saying, "Stan stood apart from us, too quiet. He sat around and smiled and puffed on his pipe. And he had a temper … wow! … a temper like a pressure cooker." But he worked very hard, she added, noting, "Stan was a loving person, love in the real sense … never from Stan did I get a sense that he didn't respect me … a person genuinely charitable toward everyone, never superficial; a person who thought deeply about things. The strength of his personality commanded respect. Nobody made snide remarks about Stan. But he was not very interesting."

The mission team's routine was to gather at the rectory for happy hour at the end of the day and afterward try to eat their evening meals together as often as possible. With 12 people present when everyone came, it was a lively and boisterous bunch. Add to that Father Carlin's frequent foreign visitors coming to experience and evaluate the mission, and it became the equivalent of hosting a dinner party almost every night. But unlike the family dinner conversations of his youth, exchanging information about friends and family and their activities — the typical and favored subjects of conversations here were theological, philosophical, academic, and anthropological, often culminating in heated clashes of opinion among members of the team. Not only was this not Stanley's cup of tea, but engaging in intellectual and hypothetical what-ifs when you could look out the window and see extreme poverty and very humble living conditions must have seemed odd, even wasteful, to Stanley's gentle and practical sensibilities.

Stanley dealt with the awkward situation by excusing himself from the group as early in the evening as possible, and basically going off by himself to his upstairs bedroom.

Lay volunteer Penny Gerbich recalled, "I remember him as being quiet and not terribly bright. I thought he was grounded. He watched. He took in. He was kind of doing studies of people and figuring out what was going on, a kind of patience."

"We were gung ho," Marcella Faudree remembered. "The spirit was strong. [Father Carlin] wanted the nuns and priests and laypeople to all work together. And I think we did for a while."

Yet what became gradually evident to Stanley was that MICATOKLA was a divided house. When it came to agreeing on an approach, purpose, and aspirations about their work with the Tz'utujil Indians and the mission, the team split into two factions. On the one hand, there was a group that believed that the goals would be better achieved with a direct, objective approach, teaching the Tz'utujil how things should be done — basically, by showing them the better, American-proven way, whether it be better farming, better education, better nutrition, better worship, or better construction.

In contrast to that was the group of missionaries who saw their role as one of assisting the Tz'utujil in their existing needs, and taking the long approach to doing so by working within the Tz'utujil culture and tradition.

"Basically, there were two philosophies," remarked Sister Elizabeth Nick. "That was the whole problem. Some thought the Indians couldn't take control and the others that they could. Were you really trying to work with the people, or to impose your views on the culture?"

Ultimately, the team had to do what MICATOKLA director Father Carlin decided. For some members of the team, the rectory building itself became a symbol of the disparity between the missionaries and the people they were serving. "Because we all lived in that big house with all those bathrooms, we became a little America right there. There simply wasn't the training of the knowledge of other cultures," Sister Elizabeth concluded. She eventually left the building and took up residence by herself in a native hut.

"There were 12 toilets on the property," noted Maryknoll Sister Linda O'Brien. "Were we evangelizing these people or were we materializing them? I began to seriously question whether what the Church was doing for those people was for their good."

Father Stafford agreed that they were not going far enough in living their missionary calling — and going too far in what and how things were introduced to the Tz'utujil community.

"When you make Indians into white middle-class people, you make drunks," he said. "Do you make them Ladinos or develop *their* culture and their richness?"

When the Sololá diocesan seminary, for example, insisted that Tz'utujil or any other indigenous candidates for the priesthood dress in Western-style clothing, Father Stafford was so angry that, as a protest, he began to wear the *traje*, the traditional Tz'utujil clothing for men. And still later on, he moved out of the rectory and into a Tz'utujil hut as a statement of disapproval regarding the mission team's overall approach.

More than once, members of the team like Montessori teacher Penny Gerbich proposed leaving the rectory for simpler quarters in town, but Father Carlin blocked that idea. Looking back on that moment decades later, Gerbich admitted that her two bright Tz'utujil assistants also disagreed with the missionaries' desire to leave the mission building, saying to them, " 'You can't go and live out in the community. You belong there [in the rectory] and people understand that.' They would have thought it odd if we had gone out and lived [in a hut] somewhere else."

As the veteran team members struggled to define their place, their mission, and their way of operating and interacting with the Santiago Atitlán community, newbie missionary Stanley stayed out of the long-winded discussions and stood by Father Carlin and Father Bob Westerman, who dismissed the arguments as a "misreading of the situation and impractical."

In those first couple of years at the Santiago mission, Father Stanley's energy was instead focused on two significant projects: helping Father Westerman's construction of a hospital building at the edge of the village — and learning two languages.

Building the *Hospitalito*

Efforts to bring quality healthcare to the Tz'utujil Maya of Santiago Atitlán became one of the Oklahoma mission team's first efforts. Not only did the people lack access to healthcare and basic health needs, but also a measles epidemic in 1964 killed more than 600 children in the town. Everything was lacking, from supplies and technical equipment to education, information, and nutrition supplements. Even as the team began to assess staff needs and programs, a building was the first priority.

Not long after arriving in Santiago, it was obvious where Father Stanley's mechanical and building skills were needed. Joining Father Westerman and two dozen Tz'utujil workers, Stanley poured his full energy and time into the hospital construction. "Stan and I laid all the concrete blocks in that building," of all 21 rooms in the main structure, Father Westerman remembered. "We worked together. We put all the inside walls up. We hand-dug the well, almost 90 feet deep. We put all the wiring in."

In a letter to Sister Marita, Stanley described to his sister how the inside walls were already completed by October 1968, and their efforts would concentrate on putting on a roof within two weeks. "Then there will be an awful lot of inside work to be done, building cabinets and shelves, doors, wiring, plumbing, etc."

Although the hospital was dedicated in July 1969, Stanley continued to labor on the building's "inside work" through 1970.

Run by mission nurses and regular rotating visiting doctors from the United States, once fully operational, Clínica Santiaguito provided the Santiago Atitlán community complete hospital services for the first time, including an operating room, lab, radiology department, and a 20-bed ward.

Building Communication

In November 1968, Stanley and two Adorers of the Blood of Christ sisters began an intensive four-month formal program in Guatemala City to learn Spanish. Sisters Marcellina Wappelhorst and Johanna Murquia had come from Wichita, Kansas, to join the Oklahoma mission as nurses for the new hospital.

The program consisted of six hours of classes and lectures, and it included extra weekends and nighttime tours and presentations on the history and culture of the Guatemalan people. Including Stanley, there were seven new priest missionaries taking the course at the Guatemalan-American Institute, so the group of men rented a large row house within walking distance of the language school.

Stanley's roommate at the house was Father James Mc-Greevy, a young priest from the Diocese of Spokane, Washington, who, like Stanley, came from a farm background.

Spanish became a 24-hour obsession for the students, remembered Father McGreevy, who even paid the shoeshine boys to polish their shoes so that they could stand there and practice their Spanish. So eager were the two men to talk and practice that it didn't take long for the price of the street lessons to jump from 5 to 25 centavos.

When the language program ended four months later, Stanley was disappointed to acknowledge that he still could not follow the speed or make out words of Ladinos speaking Spanish.

in Spanish too.... Father Carlin is happy with my progress, but of course I'm only his second student in this language.... Carlin said I should do well after 90 days.... [I]t will be worth every minute when I can go out and be able to speak with *all* the people and not just the 20 to 30 percent who know Spanish.

Stanley returned to the language school in Antigua in January 1970, but he conceded in a letter, "This is going to be a long, long process to learn it reasonably well. Right now the two cooks here, my helper and [Father] Carlin's helper are from Santiago and when I hear them speak I just hardly recognize a sound. They speak so fast."

In April 1970, Father Tom Stafford was transferred back to Oklahoma. For Stanley, this meant that his presence was needed back in Santiago Atitlán, bringing to an end his full-time study in Antigua. Yet his interest and effort to learn Tz'utujil well enough to celebrate Mass and the sacraments continued. And as Father Carlin carried on the hard work of translating the texts of the Mass and the Scripture readings into Tz'utujil, Stanley, too, continued to work to master reading and speaking each text that became available.

From first to last, "the people had more confidence in him," Sister Marcellina Wappelhorst observed. "His great asset was he could say the Mass in Tz'utujil." Years later, when asked how she'd describe Father Stanley, she said, "I would have a picture of him in his Mass vestments, or baptizing." He worked so hard that "about the only time we saw him was at the evening meal. We had a rule at the mission that in the evening we had our meal together." It included a social hour, a dinner, and a meeting, if necessary. Although Father Carlin was never successful at speaking Tz'utujil, Sister Marcellina remarked, "I think he was a great help for [Father Stanley] with the Indian language."

"Padre Francisco learned the best," noted Antonio Tzina Ratzan, who taught Tz'utujil to Father Carlin and helped create the Tz'utujil written language. "Padre Francisco worked hard and serious at the language. He would ask, 'Am I doing this right?' He learned pretty quickly."

Stanley began serving as the priest in charge at Cerro de Oro, a small mission church five miles along the lakeshore from Santiago Atitlán. All of the parishioners there were Tz'utujil Indians. "I have a parish meeting Friday night where we read over and comment on the Epistle and Gospel for Sunday," he wrote. "I do my preaching then [in Spanish], and on Sunday at Mass one of the men does the preaching [in Tz'utujil] in my place. There are 80 or more families there and they are great."

The Making of a Home

Father Stanley was so moved by the Holy Week liturgy at Cerro de Oro that he wrote a three-page handwritten letter describing it:

> Holy Thursday we had 12 men as the Apostles and [Father] Jude and I ate a meal of tortillas, fried eggs and wine at a table in the aisle [of the church].... The Good Friday services were unique too. At the moment the men read the death of Christ, a coffin was carried in and placed in the aisle. A black chasuble was placed over it

and a chalice at the head. This is to graphically show the real death of Christ the priest.

Easter Sunday morning several groups of men went to each part of town about 4 a.m. and sang "Alleluia, Christ is risen." This was the signal to come to the church for the Resurrection service. At that time the casket lid was taken off, a sheet laid inside and lilies placed around it with the paschal candle at the head.

The people elected to go back to the top of the Cerro again this year as last and it took 45 minutes to climb. It is the "hill of gold" and has special significance for them and their Mayan background. There are even timeworn stone carvings up there. We vested and just then the sun came up. All turned to the sun and adored it a few moments.... (As Father Jude Pansini later explained, the "adoring" of the sun was adoration of the risen Jesus Christ, symbolized by the sun.) We then renewed our baptismal vows by having water poured on the heads of all.... Before this, the lake was blessed from our lofty position about 1,000 feet above it.

In that same letter, Stanley mentioned for the first time a practice that he had started — and which became a trademark symbol of his love for the Tz'utujil people. Each Sunday he visited and shared a meal with a different Tz'utujil family in their hut.

By the end of Stanley's third year at the mission, the MI-CATOKLA team was completely different than the one that welcomed him in 1968. Out of the six women missionaries, only Maryknoll Sister Linda O'Brien remained. In addition to Adorers of the Blood of Christ Sisters Marcellina and Johanna, a third sister, Sister Charlotte Rohr, had come from their community to help with the new hospital.

"We held clinic six days a week, Monday through Saturday," remembered Sister Marcellina, herself an anesthetist and surgical nurse. "We were open 24 hours a day. We had one room for delivery, a nursery, and a surgical room. And we usually had patients in the big room with 13 hospital beds. It took a while to get the villagers to come, but after they came it was no problem … that was one of Father Stan's great interests."

"He had a way of getting them there. He had a talent for languages," added Sister Marcellina, without any irony. "We trained the Tz'utujil Indians for nursing and business."

Those who were acutely ill were sent to the city of Sololá or to Guatemala City. "Stan would see that they got there. He never refused," sometimes taking the patient in the back of his pickup, Sister Marcellina noted. "I think he was a person who was holy, a very prayerful person. They could come at midnight, and he would help them. He worked awfully hard, sometimes going 24 hours. He just lived it, felt every death and catastrophe."

Of the men, Fathers Tom Stafford and Jake Early were gone, and Father Bob Westerman was preparing to return to Oklahoma. Missionary work had been difficult for Father Carlin, who was now living in the city of Antigua. Although in many ways he remained Father Stanley's mentor, in the future he would have only a marginal influence on Santiago Atitlán. In 1971, Father David Iven arrived as a missionary from Oklahoma, and Benedictine Father Jude Pansini, who had left to pursue his anthropological studies, returned to Guatemala as the new director of MICATOKLA.

It was a considerably smaller group than the 12-member Oklahoma mission team, "but they had established a lot of programs and taught the Indians to carry on as best they could," Sister Marcellina explained. "I count those as the seven best years of my life. I learned so much from the people. They were such an oppressed people ... lived amidst so much suffering, yet they were so prayerful and so thankful."

When one of Father Stanley's grade school teachers came to visit the mission, he made sure that she got a good taste of daily life by experiencing a little bit of everything — including a visit to one of the remote mountain churches. "I was very impressed at the devotion of the people," Sister Clarissa Tenbrink remembered. "I fell in love with those Indian people ... so beautiful." And the "very quiet boy" named Stanley that she had taught in Okarche, she noted, had to tell her there was no place for her to work at the mission, no education spots. Sister Clarissa said she'd never forget the interaction she witnessed between Father Stanley and the Tz'utujil. "He was so sensitive to the people! He made himself a part of their life as much as possible ... and he would try to avoid anything that would offend them or hurt them in any way."

Meanwhile, back in Oklahoma, two major events there shaped Stanley's life from afar. On a personal level, his brother Jim was diagnosed with leukemia, a crisis affecting not only Jim's wife and children but also all the Rother family. In a letter to Sister Marita, 36-year-old Stanley shared his breaking heart for Jim's suffering: "Why couldn't it have been me? He has a family to provide for and it certainly isn't much of a future for them."

And in September 1971, Oklahoma's Bishop Victor Reed died suddenly from a heart attack. "He was such a good man," Stanley wrote to Sister Marita. "I have always been grateful to him for the help he gave me as a seminarian and also in the priesthood. He was always so kind and understanding. I will miss him."

On the flight back to Guatemala after Bishop Reed's funeral, Stanley's airplane flew almost directly over Lake Atitlán and the mission, giving him a firsthand view of two scenes. "I had a right window seat and got an excellent view of the town, clinic and farm from the air.... Just a bit later I noticed that the volcano Fuego had just started in eruption and a giant column of smoke and fire was belching forth." By the time he arrived in Santiago Atitlán hours later, volcanic ash began falling, covering all the roofs. The next day a hard rain settled and weighed down the volcanic material, and the roof over Stanley's bedroom collapsed — flooding the house.

The Tz'utujil People

As the number of missionaries at the mission dwindled, Stanley Rother's understanding and appreciation for the Tz'utujil people increased, aided by his developing fluency in the Tz'utujil language. The Tz'utujil are a proud people with an ancient history, one of 21 Mayan ethnic groups and 24 different ethnicities that dwell in Guatemala — a relatively small country the size of the state of Tennessee, but with 33 volcanoes. The Tz'utujil are well known for their dedication to maintaining and passing from generation to generation their cultural traditions and religious practices.

In the words of Stanley's biographer Father Monahan:

> In work, in worship, in teaching, in counseling, in home visits, in meetings, in joyful celebrations and in the saddest of times, [Father Stanley] was face-to-face or side-by-side with the Tz'utujil. Tens of thousands of encounters which poured through the fine analytic mesh of Stanley's mind collected the revealing residue of the Tz'utujil spirit.

> Tz'utujil Catholics have an unusual and striking practice of prayer during Mass. During the Eucharistic Prayer, the women cover their faces with their scarves and the men hold a hand in front of their face, like Moses hiding his face on Mount Sinai, and they all pray aloud but softly. The overall audible effect is a low hum throughout the church. To an observer these prayers seem to have a peculiar intensity. At times one can see a tear running down a cheek of a woman. Although Stanley and the other Oklahoma missionaries realized this custom went beyond standard liturgical practice, none of them ever tried to forbid it. Those murmured prayers of the poor Tz'utujil clearly touched Stanley's heart.[15]

Gradually but noticeably, Stanley became deeply influenced by the impoverishment of the Tz'utujil people, which affected his attitude toward material things and challenged him to live a simpler lifestyle. "Christmas has always been a little hard here," he wrote to Sister Marita in 1972. "Following American customs doesn't seem right among a people who can't give or receive anything because of their poverty. [Father] Jude wants turkey, trimmings, lights and the whole bit, but for me that isn't important. I already have been invited to eat in one of the poorer homes in town."

Stanley found it easier to speak to the Tz'utujil, who spoke Spanish more slowly, than to the Ladinos — and as his fluency in Tz'utujil increased, he would switch to or answer in Tz'utujil even when the conversation began in Spanish. He also came to know the Tz'utujil through the fellowship of shared manual labor, whether on the farm, at the clinic, or at the church. "We would work the land," Diego Coché recalled. They cleared the fields of stones, planted, nurtured, and harvested corn, black beans, potatoes, and garbanzo beans. "Padre Francisco would keep us going when we were down. He would say, 'God is with us.'"

Stanley found himself "pulled emotionally to the side of the Tz'utujil rather than the Ladinos," Father Monahan wrote. "There were about 30 Tz'utujil to every one Ladino in Santiago Atitlán, but the Ladinos had been deeply inculturated to consider themselves superior. So we find this mildly sarcastic comment in a letter to Sister Marita about a fiesta. 'They always have two queens and of course the Ladino Queen is the most important.' This bit of prejudice may have been abetted by Stanley's mentor Ramon Carlin. A visitor to the village recalled walking up a rocky path with Carlin as a Ladino boy approached from the opposite direction. 'Here comes a member of the master race,' growled Carlin. 'I.Q. 80.'"[16]

One of the most unusual and unique practices of the Tz'utujil culture is the *cofradía*, or confraternity, a unique group that combines Mayan roots and the country's Catholic history. Not well understood by the United States missionaries when they first arrived in Guatemala, it contributed to the division in opinion on how to engage with the community, and how to present the Catholic faith to the Tz'utujil.

When the Oklahomans arrived at Santiago Atitlán in 1964, they quickly learned that the *cofradías* were strong local religious groups with devotion to the many *santos* found along the walls of the ancient church. The missionaries also discovered, to their shock, that the *cofradías* held in their possession the actual keys to the church!

Dating back to the 16th century in Spain, *cofradías* were originally a sort of guild system that evolved into religious confraternities or brotherhoods, each responsible for the care of an image of its patron saint and the celebration of his feast day. During the Counter-Reformation, they became very popular as mediums for explaining the Catholic faith. Once the concept transferred to the New World, *cofradías* became tools for the Spanish friars for the propagation of the Catholic faith to the Indians.

According to historical accounts, in Santiago Atitlán the *cofradías* were probably in full operation by 1585. By organizing the newly converted Indians into eight or 10 *cofradías* — each under the patronage of a Catholic saint (San Juan Bautista, Santiago, Santa María del Rosario) or a mystery (Santísimo Sacramento, Santa Cruz); each with its set of officials responsible for the group's activities — the friars simplified the task of carrying out the liturgical and para-liturgical celebrations of the Church's liturgical year. *Cofrades*, as *cofradía* members are called, probably also served as the choir, participating with the friars in the chanting of the Divine Office and the Mass. They were responsible for the regular care of the Church and its numerous statues, the cleaning and replacement of candles and similar services.

Unfortunately, once the Spanish — and with them, the friars — left the remote region around Lake Atitlán, what followed was a period of several centuries without the consistent presence of a priest and/or Catholic influence. Over time, the *cofradías* developed various *costumbres*, or traditions, that seemed to carry a double meaning: Christian on the surface with Mayan symbolism underneath. Something that most likely began as a form of teaching the Catholic faith evolved into influential groups providing social and economic services.

Any 20th-century foreign missionary to Guatemala had to decide if and how to address this unfamiliar organization — and Stanley was no exception. To make things more complicated, at that time there existed a clear division between the *cofradías* and Acción Católica, or Catholic Action. Most Tz'utujil belonged to one or the other, but not to both, in spite of the fact that historically both groups developed in the 20th century side-by-side.

The Oklahomans' interest in *cofradías* reached a new level when the missionaries became aware of Maximón, a squat figure with a wooden face accentuated by a long cigar in its mouth. In Santiago Atitlán, the effigy of Maximón is kept in various houses during the course of a year, and it is ceremonially moved during the grand *Semana Santa* (Holy Week) procession. Although Maximón played a central role in the rituals of the *cofradía*, it did not represent any historical Catholic saint. The Oklahoma team concluded that he must be a Mayan idol — and Father Carlin ordered all the missionaries to have nothing to do with the *co-fradía*, and especially Maximón.

Yet Father Carlin did not go to war with the *cofradía*, allowing it to continue its real but peripheral role in the worship of the parish, especially during Holy Week. Whenever Father Carlin met the *cabecera*, or head of the *cofradía*, for example, they would give each other a hearty, Latino-style bear hug.

"Maximón was not allowed in the church building," recollected Sister Marcellina Wappelhorst, a member of the Adorers of the Blood of Christ community and a native of St. Charles, Missouri. Sister Marcellina remembered that, "One of our best men in the clinic was in a *cofradía*.... I think ultimately [Stanley] tolerated them and their practices."

By all accounts, Stanley was intrigued by the *cofradía* and its traditions, and he seemed to see it as an ingenious attempt to hold connections to their Mayan past. But above all, Stanley appeared interested in making sure that the Tz'utujil did not consider their Mayan roots and connections as evil, wanting to purify and incorporate what was good in the *cofradía* traditions and practices into orthodox Catholicism. Insofar as his conscience would allow, Stanley cooperated with the *cofradía* and befriended their individual members.

Hella Jaenike de De Paz, a German missionary in the Lake Atitlán region who worked with the radio ministry, remembered Stanley participating in the Good Friday processions, even walking with the *cofradía*. "He was the man who tried to know the people ... went to their houses ... tried to understand them. He gave himself completely to the people here. It was very beautiful." Padre Francisco, she emphasized, "followed his conscience. His heart was good. He is a holy martyr."

"I got a lot of inspiration from [Stanley] about relations with the *cofradía*," noted Baton Rouge priest David Vavasseur, who was stationed at a nearby mission. "I can recall [Stan and the missionaries] even going to meetings of the *cofradía* ... we came a long way from having just a bunch of drunks on our hands to some of the *cofradía* becoming some of our best catechists."

On December 7, 1965, Pope Paul VI promulgated *Ad Gentes*, the Second Vatican Council's Decree on the Mission Activity of the Church, which stated: "Whatever good is found to be sown in the hearts and minds of men, or in the rites and cultures peculiar to various peoples, not only is not lost, but is healed, uplifted, and perfected for the glory of God, the shame of the demon, and the bliss of men" (n. 9).

Whether consciously following this document or not, it is clear that Padre Francisco was living its truth with zeal at the Oklahoma mission of Santiago Apóstol at Santiago Atitlán.

Back in Oklahoma, 42-year-old Californian John R. Quinn was ordained as the fifth bishop of the Diocese of Oklahoma City and Tulsa in 1971. A year later, the 67-year-old Diocese of Oklahoma City and Tulsa was divided into two — Tulsa becoming it's own diocese and John Quinn becoming the first archbishop of Oklahoma City. But Santiago Atitlán continued to be an official mission of the whole state, in spite of it now being under the governance of two bishops.

And Then There Was One: MICATOKLA Changes

Although he was officially the director of MICATOKLA, Benedictine monk Jude Pansini found his missionary passion out in the fincas, the coffee and cardamom plantations in the mountains behind the village of Santiago Atitlán. "They are distressing places," he wrote. "The silent violence of exploitation" which kills, especially children. Father Pansini spent the majority of his time and energy ministering to the Tz'utujil living in barracks and working in horrible conditions — while fighting for health care and better living conditions in what was a desperate situation for people living even more impoverished than the average Tz'utujil living in town. There were four principal fincas around Santiago, all under the care of the Oklahoma mission: Olas de Moca, Monte de Oro, Metzabal, and Montequina.

"The people on the fincas were really in bad shape. They were really pale," stated Dr. John Emrich, who served in the mission for eight years, along with his wife, Susan, and their two children. "I ran the health program," which included the hospital, the nutrition center, the field clinic in Cerro de Oro, and the children's clinic in town. "Father Stanley and I worked together. I saw him a lot. He had a lot of heart and soul, a good sense of what is right … he was a very generous man. You don't find many people who are dedicated like that."

With Father Pansini spending three to four days a week in the fincas, responsibility for the pastoral care of Santiago Atitlán fell upon Father Stanley. In addition to the mission's liturgical and sacramental duties, he became responsible for the mission's finances. Stanley also spent a considerable amount of time training and teaching catechists. And of course, he continued to put his mechanical know-how to good use, serving as maintenance and repairman for the mission's vehicles, the church, the rectory, and even the hospital.

But the transformations taking place at the mission became much bigger than merely who was taking care of what. In 1974, Father Jude Pansini left the mission of Santiago Atitlán. In 1975, Father David Iven also went away — leaving only Father Stanley to run the Oklahoma operation, a far cry from the staff of 12 that made up MICATOKLA when he arrived in 1968.

To make matters worse, looking at it from a distance in Oklahoma, the Guatemala mission seemed to lack foundation — and to be suffering from some form of communal identity crisis. While we may never understand all the social and cultural difficulties that affected and distressed this community of lay volunteers and priests, the concluding statistics are nevertheless shocking.

Of the six priests who were assigned to the Guatemala mission when Stanley arrived, four had walked away from the priesthood by the mid-1970s — two of them were diocesan priests, and the other two religious-order priests, one a Benedictine and the other a Jesuit. The two mission priests who remained true to their priestly vocation were Father Stanley and Father Carlin. But even Father Carlin's situation was cause for concern. Although he had returned to Oklahoma in 1972, "he felt like a forgotten man in the Oklahoma diocese after returning from Guatemala, and the loneliness when it surfaced was made worse by the fact that he had left his heart there," wrote editor Jeanne Devlin for the *Sooner Catholic*.[17] In the final years of his life, however, Father Carlin sought psychotherapeutic treatment, regaining emotional health and finding peace as the pastor of a small rural church until his death.[18]

Yet the damage to the mission's public image had been done. It didn't help matters that when the Oklahoma diocese split into two dioceses, the financial consequence of that event meant there was no diocesan newspaper in either diocese to inform the Church of Oklahoma about the people who were serving in its Guatemala mission — or that the diocesan Mission Board that had served as guide and monitor to the project appears to have basically faded away.

The bottom line was that Oklahomans didn't know much about the Church's mission in Guatemala during this time period, and the mission itself was lacking vision and struggling both spiritually and financially. As Father Stanley reflected in a letter dated August 1973: "Our money for fiscal 73-74 had another cut this year, from 51,000 last year to about 37,000 this year. This isn't going to be easy to stay with."

What is undoubtedly providential is the fact that precisely in the midst of this troubled situation, Father Stanley Rother not only remained certain about his vocation, but he also cemented his conviction as a missionary. He knew with complete confidence that he had found the place and the people where God's providence willed him to be.

"I guess change is good after a while, but between us I hope I'm not up for a change in the near future," he wrote to Sister Marita. "This kind of work, I hope, will be given special consideration for length of tenure. Maybe they'll let me retire here," he concluded. "I would stay if all support from Oklahoma were stopped. The [Rother family] farm may have to support me some day."

CHAPTER 5

Padre Francisco

The first time Oklahoma City Archbishop John Quinn visited MICATOKLA in 1975, "the volcano was fuming and there was a lot of ash. It would get caught in the bottom of your pants," recalled his companion, Father Thomas Boyer. "At night you could see the strips of lava flowing." Overwhelmed by the physical beauty of the place, Father Boyer also remembered being incredibly impressed by Father Stanley's endurance in a place where the unexpected is always normal. But in a special way, he was impressed by Father Stanley's patience and serenity toward the people and their needs. "There was no rush," people would come in and "he would stop and listen. He would always be present to them; sometimes he'd pull a piece of paper from his shirt pocket and write a note to himself," Father Boyer recalled. "There was a gentle graciousness there."

Father Boyer, who joked that he was invited to go to Guatemala by Archbishop Quinn "to carry the luggage," recalled seeing a level of poverty that he'd never seen before in his many travels. This was a place where everything was primitive, rudimentary — like the one light bulb in the whole town, located in the town square by the church.

Father Stanley carried out hours of work at the big dining room table, Father Boyer remembered, using it "very much like an office. There was a stream of people that came through, and he'd just listen to everyone, one by one, and write things down."

Father Stanley's vision regarding the purpose and function of the Oklahoma mission, as well as his increasing understanding about his vocation as a missionary, was evident in his actions. "He didn't go there to do anything. He went there to *be* there, with the people," Father Boyer emphasized. "And because he was there, other things happened ... like the school, and the clinic, and farming the fields."

The Missionary's Work of Love

And the people responded to Father Stanley, frequently seeking advice, a helping hand, or material assistance. As he wrote to Sister Marita in a letter dated August 1973: "Almost all evenings there are one, two or three visitors or [others who] come on business and then lights are out [at 10 p.m.], and I go to bed." It was no happenstance that a sign in Father Stanley's office declared: "Work is love made visible," a quote by poet Khalil Gibran. Whatever they needed, noted parishioner Cristóbal Coché Atzip, they knew Father Stanley would begin by listening: "Whenever the people were hungry, he gave them food. Whenever they needed money ... whenever there was an emergency, they would come to him first, because they could trust him."

Just presiding over the mission's liturgical life — something he was now doing completely on his own — demanded a unique understanding and imaginative vision from Father Stanley. The numbers alone required resourcefulness. In

1974, for example, there were 649 babies baptized at Lake Atitlán; approximately 2,000 Holy Communions were distributed each week; 85 couples made marriage vows at a group ceremony during the village's annual Fiesta; and about 150 little ones came forward for their First Communion.

Father Stanley decided that the past presidents of the leading parish organization, Acción Católica, who were also trained as extraordinary ministers of Holy Communion, were the obvious group to bring the Eucharist to the sick and homebound. In a May 1974 letter to Sister Marita, he wrote: "Today I sent four of them out to each zone in town to take communion to the sick. [The village is divided into seven zones, or cantons]. We wrote a formulary for them to use and they are sent out in my name and the name of the people present. I sent them right after Communion of the Mass. I'm just not able to do all of this myself."

In addition to pastoral duties, Father Stanley continued to hold dear and devote himself to the 110 acres of co-op farmland south of the village owned by the mission, where he was combination farm boss and agricultural guide. "About two-thirds of the farm is divided now into parcels and farmed by sharecroppers [45 men were involved]," wrote Father Stanley, in an April 1973 letter to Sister Marita. Ever the farmer, he explained:

> They will have to follow certain requirements such as type and amount of fertilizer used, use of organic matter and green manure. Hopefully they will realize better yields and will use these same methods on their own land and also encourage others, too. I have three new types of corn I am trying this year and also will try

more wheat, soybeans etc.... I still want to find a better variety of corn and also some other cash crop that will do good. We have lowered the infant mortality rate by our medical programs, and now there are more mouths to feed.

Whether wheat, corn, or even garlic, Father Stanley's farming efforts were carried out shoulder to shoulder with the Tz'utujil farmers. "We worked together on the finca a lot. We planted beans, tomatoes, and other things," Nicolás Chávez Culan said. "A lot of men cooperated with him. We worked in the field, and we came in here and worked two or three hours in the church." As is true anywhere, the farming news was not always good: "The weather here is sure making a bad situation worse," Father Stanley wrote in 1974. "Most people planted their corn early and the rains started on schedule in May and the crops looked good. Then the rains stopped around July 1, and very little corn put on ears. All is now drying up and falling over. The price of fertilizer has more than doubled since last year and was too high to buy ... the black beans had a hard time too and most didn't bear. There are going to be a lot of hungry people this year."

Oklahoma volunteer Mary Tinker remembered how Father Stanley loved to visit the fincas, and did so frequently: "He did love the Tz'utujil people, more than he did the Ladinos; his heart just went out to them. When he went to the fincas, the people would kiss his hands," noted Mary, who was a regular volunteer at the mission along with her husband, Joe. When in Santiago, the Tinkers lived in the rectory compound and assisted Father

Stanley with manual work, sharing meals and the quiet evening hours. "There are a lot of 'Franciscos' in Santiago Atitlán as a result of Stan," Joe laughed, adding: "I think his whole life was one big prayer ... even when he got mad at the people.... I don't think he held a grudge against any of them."

"He liked to laugh," Mary mentioned. "He had a good time with the natives ... he would just laugh and talk with them." Father Stanley had a "good sense of humor," she added, and loved to tease Mary about her reaction to the unexpected and unusual events of life in a mission — like driving through a wall of water in an uncovered Bronco. Father Stanley teased her so much, she said, that she would tell him, "Father, you're going to have to go to confession!"

Perhaps the one custom that best exemplifies Father Stanley's heartfelt desire for genuine community with the Tz'utujil was his tradition of home visits and shared meals. In addition to learning their challenging language, Father Stanley made a practice of visiting individual families every week, rotating cantons, or neighborhoods, with each visit. With anywhere from 50 to 100 couples exchanging vows at each summer Fiesta, these visits became a major part of his ministry. But what a beautiful ritual it was. At each home, he blessed their simple dirt-floor dwelling, shared the meal, and presented the couple with a photograph of themselves at their wedding. In an August 1975 letter to Sister Marita, 40-year-old Stanley explained, "It is quite satisfying and revealing: satisfying for the contact and interest, and revealing as to the poverty that exists so close to us here and the great faith and spirit they manifest. Maybe it does me more good than it does them."

It was important to Father Stanley that these home visits retain the simplicity and authenticity of a shared Eucharistic moment, so he emphasized to the host family his desire to be served the same food that they ate. Cristóbal Coché Atzip, one of the many parishioners who fondly recalled those special meals, remarked, "Padre Francisco was one of our own. He ate what the people ate. If they ate weeds, he ate weeds. If they ate fish, he ate fish."

Retired Kansan Frankie Williams was a yearly volunteer at the Santiago Atitlán mission. At her very first visit, Frankie remembered Father Stanley inviting her to accompany him on his sick calls, something he did almost every night after dinner. "He invited me to go to see this fellow who was dying," she said, describing the dark night and their walk that began downhill, and how Father Stanley worried about her falling. He looked over and said to Frankie, "Here, take my arm ... we had to climb these real steep steps, maybe 15 of them." During the visit, Frankie sat on a stool as Father Stanley did everything he normally did. When they started walking back, she said, Father Stanley kindly let her know how well she handled her first house visit, and he did so partly by teasing Frankie about her difficulty walking. From then on, "Every time he went on a sick call when I was there, he took me with him."

One particular home visit that stood out in Frankie Williams' mind was to a dying man named Tomás, who was known throughout Santiago Atitlán as "the bishop." Tomás was "like a thermometer of the village," Frankie described, "and he shared a lot of that with Stan." Tomás used to walk behind Father Stanley in the public processions.

When they arrived at Tomás' hut that evening, they knew that "the bishop" was dying. Frankie sat on a small chair and prayed while Father Stanley reached out to anoint him. All of a sudden, as if he'd been given a shot of energy, "Tomás said something out loud in Tz'utujil and raised up to a sitting position while being anointed … he put his hands on Stan's head and started to pray in Tz'utujil." When he finished, Tomás just fell back. "At that point Stan looked at me, and I could see his eyes watering," she remembered. Frankie was crying outside the hut as she waited for Father Stanley to come out. When he saw Frankie, Father Stanley handed her his handkerchief, and they began to walk away together. "I said, 'Stan, what did he say?' He said, 'Frankie, I can't tell you. I would be too embarrassed, and besides, I hope it doesn't happen.' Without a doubt," Williams added, that night in Tomás hut "was one of the most profound experiences of my life."

As he did with Frankie, when his friends, family, or other volunteers came to visit the mission, Father Stanley frequently invited the guests to join him on the home visits to his parishioners, allowing them a personal opportunity to experience on their own the Tz'utujil people he came to love and serve. Father Stanley's second-grade teacher, Sister Flora Jentgen, who had worked at a poor mission in Brazil far up the Amazon River before arriving in Santiago Atitlán, remembered how startled she was by the experience. There was "a stark reality" to their homes. "The food was just unbelievable poverty," she noted. They sat on tiny wooden chairs. A single candle provided the light. "After Father Rother said a blessing, the father of the family said a blessing. Then everyone rinsed their mouths out with water and spit in the corner!"

But these home visits were also physically difficult on Father Stanley in ways that he would not readily admit. Aurea Albiso Merida, a Ladino woman who for 25 years operated the Casa Bonita for badly malnourished children at the mission, said about Father Stanley: "He would visit all the people. He would always eat with everyone around here. He got sick lots of times. I would tell him, you are sick and you cannot eat what they have, but he could not tell them and hurt their feelings."

Perhaps he could have been more careful, or been more faithful about taking gamma globulin shots (to build up his immunity), as former mission nurse Marcella Faudree used to nag him to do. But in a very real way, it was inevitable that Father Stanley would join the long roster of missionaries who became ill while serving the Church in Guatemala and other places with similarly poor and unsanitary conditions.

"As I write this, the lawn outside my window is a pretty green, a multitude of flowers in bloom and a humming bird makes daily visits to the flowers nearby," wrote Father Stanley to his sister in a letter dated August 1972. "My room is a basement room in this building and as I sit in my raised bed my eye level is that of the grass. In my left arm is a needle and plastic hose draining glucose into my veins — a quart a day. Yes, this is a hospital and my room is in solitary confinement or isolation. I have an illness called infectious hepatitis."

Although it is a difficult thing for everyone, learning to take care of oneself as a missionary in the midst of such dire and extreme conditions has to inevitably carry its own unique set of

Father Stanley Francis Rother, 1975, the year he became the sole missionary at the Oklahoma mission (photo by Father David Monahan; all photos courtesy of the Rother family or the Archdiocese of Oklahoma City Archives unless otherwise noted).

School Days
1946-47

A young Stanley on the steps of the Rother farmhouse porch. Inset: Eleven-year-old Stanley, a fifth-grader at Holy Trinity School.

Franz and Gertrude Rother at their Okarche farmhouse with their children. Left to right: Elizabeth Mary (Betty Mae), Jim, Tom, and Stanley (c. 1944).

Stanley as an altar boy at Holy Trinity Church, Okarche. Inset: Stanley's senior year photo, 1953. The yearbook that year was dedicated to Our Lady of Fátima.

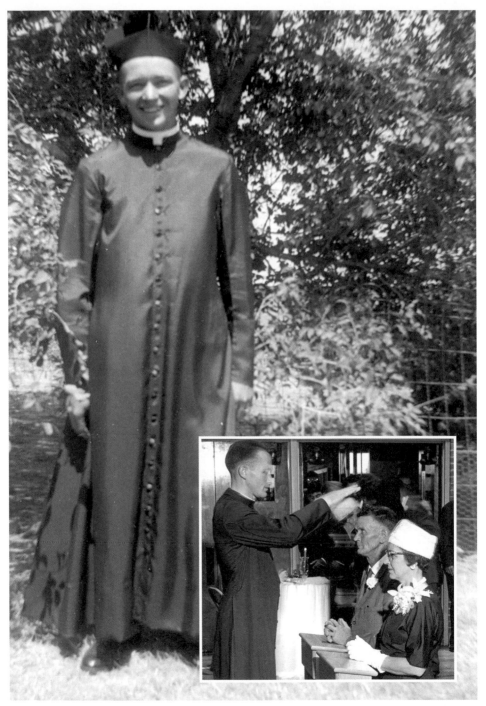

Seminarian Stanley Rother dressed for classes (photo courtesy of the Rother family). Inset: Immediately following Stanley's ordination, Gertrude and Franz Rother kneel before their oldest child to receive his blessing, May 25, 1963. Stanley was one of 11 men ordained that year by Bishop Victor Reed for the Diocese of Oklahoma City and Tulsa.

Twenty-eight–year-old Father Stanley Rother with his parents on the day of his first Mass, May 26, 1963, celebrated at his home parish of Holy Trinity in Okarche.

Rother family portrait (c. 1970). Back row, left to right: Tom, Sister Marita (Betty Mae), and Jim. *Front row, left to right*: Father Stanley, Gertrude, and Franz.

At the age of 33, Father Stanley became an Oklahoma missionary to the Tz'utujil community of Santiago Atitlán, on the shores of Lake Atitlán, Guatemala.

Children felt a natural affinity for Father Stanley. It was not unusual for him to have a trail of giggling children following him and grabbing his hands.

Blessing a Tz'utujil baby.

The parish church in Santiago Atitlán, St. James the Apostle, at the time of Father Stanley Rother.

Enjoying coffee with religious sisters, both mission volunteers.

Celebrating Mass at one of the four fincas, the coffee and cardamom mountain plantations behind the village of Santiago Atitlán, all of which were under the care of the Oklahoma mission. He loved to visit the fincas, and did so regularly.

Father Stanley with his associate pastor, Father Pedro Bocel, a full-blooded Cakchiquel Indian, 1981 (photo by Frankie Williams).

Father Stanley never stopped the practice of visiting his parishioners, no matter how remote or how difficult the roads.

With a group of young parishioners — including a boy he took to Guatemala City to be treated and cured of a lip cancer, January 1981 (photo by Frankie Williams).

Gertrude and Franz Rother welcome their son as he arrives safely in Oklahoma City on January 29, 1981, after fleeing Guatemala following death threats (photo by Father David Monahan).

Franz and Gertrude Rother leaving a Memorial Mass for their son at their home parish, Holy Trinity Church, in Okarche, Oklahoma, August 2, 1981.

Rother family gathered at Holy Trinity Catholic Cemetery, August 3, 1981.

The decorations that had been put up for the parish and town Fiesta in honor of St. James were still up when the casket holding the pastor of the Tz'utujil was brought into the large, overcrowded church in Santiago Atitlán. Someone donated wood to build the custom-sized coffin. None of the coffins in town were long enough to fit Father Stanley's long, thin frame.

As a compromise with the Rother family, Father Stanley's body was sent to Oklahoma to be buried, but his heart and his blood remained in the Santiago Atitlán church, where he belonged. Two large jars, one containing Father Stanley's blood and the other the pastor's bloody gauze, were ceremonially processed in and placed on the altar for the Mass, next to a metal box holding the martyr's heart.

The room where Father Stanley was murdered is now a parish chapel. The bullet that was most likely responsible for his death went through Father Stanley's skull and is still lodged in the floor (photo courtesy of María Ruiz Scaperlanda).

Father Stanley F. Rother (1935–1981), martyr from Oklahoma.

challenges. In Father Stanley's own words, written toward the end of the same letter to Sister Marita: "We are to spend ourselves for Christ, but then there is prudence involved too. We are no good for anything if we have no health. I may have let my resistance get too low and may have contributed to my condition now." At the end of the three-page letter, Father Stanley added a curious and funny postscript to his beloved sister: "Wash your hands good after reading this; just in case."

One of the Carmelite sisters who served at the parish remembered when Father Stanley received a check for $500 in a letter, with a note that said the money was a gift for him to buy new clothes. "He said, 'I don't need clothes. The ones who need it are the poor people … put that money in the account for the people,' " she remembered.

Simplicity was his lifestyle, Sister Marita agreed, and she felt challenged by his sincere austerity. "He helped me.… I thought I was living a simple life. But after a summer in Guatemala, I knew that I could be doing a better job in living simply!"

Father Stanley dressed very humbly, Aurea Albiso Merida remembered, and he carried his pipe in a shirt pocket, "even though he didn't smoke it all that much. Even now I can still smell the odor of Padre Francisco's pipe." Father Stanley liked to end each day in the rectory's living room, reading the Guatemala City newspaper or *Time* magazine, and lighting up his pipe.

Family Bonds Across the Miles

Knowing that Jim Rother's cancer was serious, Stanley was deliberate about visiting his younger brother in Oklahoma as

much as he could. On one of her first visits to the mission, Sister
Marita remembers giving an update to her big brother about
Jim, and about the difficult and painful journey that Jim and his
family were suffering. Because it was near Jim's birthday, Father
Stanley decided to drive for several hours to Guatemala City so
that he and Sister Marita could get to a phone and call Jim together. "For some reason I was reflecting on that recently," Sister
Marita said. "And how tender it was of Stanley, what a soft heart
he had for his family. It was good for me to see that … I saw a
tenderness in Stanley at that time that I had never been exposed
to before."

The following year, on February 1, 1974, Jim finally lost his
battle to leukemia, leaving behind a young wife, Mary Lou, and
two boys, 9-year-old Kenneth and 7-year-old Matt. It must have
been extremely difficult for Father Stanley to be so far away
from his family when it happened — and to not be able to attend Jim's funeral. In a letter to Sister Marita, dated February 28,
he wrote:

> It doesn't seem possible that Jim has been gone for a
> month already. I was upset that word didn't get to me
> in time, but I was with him just a scant 18 days earlier.
> Don's telegram got here at 10:30 a.m. Sunday and the
> last plane to get me there in time left Guate [Guatemala
> City] at 12 noon. Dave suggested I go on anyway even
> if I was late, but I didn't like that idea at all.
>
> Anyway, it just wasn't supposed to be any other way. To
> me it just isn't that important to be present for such an

occasion. But of course listening to all the comments of relatives and other concerned persons, 'Oh how awful' or 'what a shame'! But why do we have to conform ourselves to the expectations of others? To me, Jim is in Heaven. It would have been nice to be present for his Mass and burial, but distance and conditions made it impossible. I don't feel it is that necessary to put on a good show. If we treat death as the passage to a greater life, why all the fuss for the body?

The next year, Franz and Gertrude Rother went to visit their son Stanley in Guatemala for the second time, this time joining him for the elaborate celebration of Holy Week — and participating in everything with him. On Holy Saturday, Franz even joined his son in a procession, for which the *cofradía* presented Franz with one of their distinctive scarves to wear. Father Stanley and his father also participated in the procession's ritual drinking of "moonshine." As Father Stanley described it in a letter to Sister Marita: "[Dad] will have many happy memories of that occasion" and "the folks thoroughly enjoyed Holy Week here."

In addition to the regular correspondence between Father Stanley and Sister Marita, the two siblings were able to enjoy a considerable number of face-to-face encounters both in Guatemala and in Oklahoma, getting together when Father Stanley visited Oklahoma on business or vacation, and when Sister Marita was able to volunteer at Santiago Atitlán. She went twice to the mission representing her community, the Adorers of the Blood of Christ, who had a regular presence at the mission. "One time I worked with another sister at the nutrition center, and out at the hospital where we did laundry," she recalled. "Stanley did take time to show me some things. We took a small plane ride, out to the Mayan ruins in Tikal — and I drove out to the outlying missions with him where he had Masses."

In the summer of 1975, Sister Marita, Father Stanley, and another sister made the long drive from Oklahoma to Guatemala in a new vehicle for the mission. "We went to Mexico City. We saw the pyramids. He loved history and historical things, so it was a highlight for him to get to show it and tell us about it." Sister Marita stayed for five weeks in Santiago to help with the indexing of baptismal and marriage registries at the parish.

Looking back now, Sister Marita says that their time together in Guatemala provided them with the best quality time they had ever had as adults. "I gained such a great appreciation about what he was doing, to see him among the people and to see why he liked it, to see how much he liked being there.... He seemed so at peace with the people, who would stop and talk to him, and how the kids loved him," Sister Marita said, smiling. "Just seeing all of that was such a rewarding experience, so that I could picture him like that all of the time! Before that, I really had no idea about what he was going through."

Perhaps more than any other record of his time in Guatemala, Father Stanley's regular correspondence with Sister Marita offers a glimpse into the missionary's heart that goes far beyond information. It is through his letters that we often hear the profundity of his faith, and his growing love for the Tz'utujil people who became intimate family to him.

Living a Eucharistic Life

Every day, when it came time for the midday meal, Father Stanley opened the rectory door and welcomed *el Viejo* Nicolás, an elderly indigent Tz'utujil man. No one knows how or what brought Father Stanley to begin this practice, but for more than six years — until Nicolás' death — Father Stanley invited "Old Man" Nicolás to be his guest and sit to his left at the table. Every day, Father Stanley leaned over to cut Nicolás' meat, and he carried on with the rhythm of the meal as if there was nothing unusual or unpleasant about it. In truth, not everyone who visited or shared the dining table with them appreciated Nicolás' presence, his body odor, or his inability to use eating utensils. Aurea Albiso Merida, who used to cook on a regular basis at the rectory, described Nicolás as "an old man, very dirty," who ate lunch with Padre Francisco on a daily basis.

Many urged Father Stanley to have the old man and his disgusting manners sit at another table. Instead, day after day, Father Stanley sat him at his elbow and carried on the daily practice, as if it was the most normal thing in the world. At the end of the meal, Father Stanley encouraged Nicolás to take a nap on one of the rectory's beds before heading home. "Padre Francisco would also give him food to take home to his son," Aurea added.

Bishop Angélico Melotto of the Diocese of Sololá recalled hearing about Father Stanley's tradition. "He always had a poor beggar eating lunch with him. That impressed me. Sometimes we think of the Americans as too elegant."

Despite his increasing responsibilities, Father Stanley was anything but a stereotypical "American." Manuel Reanda, who worked with Father Stanley as a catechist and served as president of Acción Católica, remembered the young priest as someone who preached with his actions, not merely with his words: "The one who worked the hardest with us was Padre Francisco … from the day he arrived until the day he died. When he organized us as catechists, if it hadn't been for Padre Francisco I wouldn't be able to read."

Above all the tributes he could say about his close friend Father Stanley, Diego Coché said he is most grateful for the fact that Father Stanley encouraged Diego's son Cristóbal to consider and to go to the seminary. "The main thing was my son in the seminary…. My son will be ordained because of Padre Francisco," Diego said after Father Stanley's death. Although Father Stanley often helped Diego and Francisca Quic and their family of eight children, for Diego, nothing compares to the fact that Father Stanley affirmed with confidence that his son Cristóbal, the only Tz'utujil in the seminary at the time, had a vocation to the priesthood.

During Cristóbal's years in the seminary, Father Stanley visited him to see that he had what he needed. Looking back on those years now, Father Cristóbal Coché admitted he's not sure what would have happened if Father Stanley hadn't invited him to the seminary — and Cristóbal regrets that Father Stanley died before he was ordained. "He never knew that I was going to be a Benedictine priest," Father Cristóbal added.

Over time, Father Stanley became friendly with a tall Tz'utujil man named Nicolás Chivilui, a well-known elder in Santiago, who was recognized as a powerful shaman and who also held a high position in the *cofradía*. At some point, Chivilui began the ritual of dropping by the rectory with a couple of bottles of beer so that he and Father Stanley would have a chance to chat together as they drank. In a letter dated March 1977, Father Stanley wrote:

> An old gentleman, says he's 90, came in Sunday morning during breakfast and told me he wants to get his marriage blessed. His nephew is president of Catholic Action now and has talked to him. It is interesting because he has spent his whole life as the traditional witch doctor here and people come to him from all over to have him pray for their intentions, and I've noticed recently they end their rounds of the saints with a Mass.... I'll probably have his wedding this Sunday.

The *cofradía* had already honored Father Stanley with scarves marking their distinctive membership. And Chivilui's marriage blessing was one more public sign of the friendly relations between Father Stanley the pastor and the *cofradía*. It was the *cofradía* that bestowed Father Stanley with the distinguished Tz'utujil name of Apla's.

It was characteristic of Father Stanley to stop at nearby San Lucas and have a cup of coffee with fellow missionary Father Gregory Schaffer. "His growth was particularly admirable in the way he grew in appreciation, love, and understanding of the people ... his understanding of [the Tz'utujil] was uncanny ... he probably had as good an understanding of the Indian people in their thinking and actions as anyone around. It showed itself in gentleness, patience, firmness," said Father Schaffer. "He was incredible speaking the Tz'utujil language.

Stan's understanding of the language reflected his understanding of the people."

Although he met Father Stanley as a young boy when the missionary priest came to eat with his family at their home, Diego Chávez Culan said that later, when he was a teenager, his "way of life" took him "away from Padre Francisco. I had a vice. I used to drink a lot." Yet in the late 1970s, Diego remembered "meeting" Father Stanley again, "and we became very good friends. He spoke to me in Tz'utujil. He knew me very well. He offered me a chance to be a lector, and from then on I would come in to him and he would tell me the readings for each week. He would teach me how to read the Scriptures in Tz'utujil, and I learned a lot. I remember exactly the first time I read — April 29, 1979."

Salvador Atzip Sosof also remembered meeting Father Stanley when Salvador was a child. "When I was young, we played outside [the rectory], and he was always talking with us." Father Stanley liked children a lot, Salvador recalled. "I always remember him speaking in Tz'utujil, and he was very happy with us. He encouraged us to come to catechism to learn about Jesus Christ." When he visited Salvador's home, "he blessed the house. [My parents] gave him a glass of coffee and a piece of bread, and he was very happy."

When he walked up to young Tz'utujil males, Father Stanley had the habit of giving them a strong macho punch to the upper arm, along with his smile or a laugh. Salvador, who was 17 at his wedding, remembered Father Stanley speaking in the ceremony about St. James and the apostle's martyrdom, "then we went to confession one by one. Afterwards he gave us a remembrance, a diploma [marriage certificate], and a medal," which Father Stanley blessed. He told Salvador that the medal was to remind him of his Mother Mary, "and not to forget that," added Salvador, who said he also kept a keepsake cross given to him by Padre Francisco from the day of his confirmation.

For Father Marvin Leven, two images stood out from his visits to Santiago Atitlán. No matter how long or where they had been, when he and Father Stanley rode back into town, the joyful welcome always included greeting shouts of "Apla's! Apla's!" — a unique and very personal experience. In addition, Father Stanley instilled in his parishioners a deliberate and distinct understanding of service to others through tithing. On Sundays, everybody put a penny in the collection. And every Thursday at Mass, a plastic cloth was spread in front of the altar. As people came in, they all contributed food to share with the poor, so that by the end, there was a big stack of corn and beans on the plastic.

As a U.S. volunteer noted, "He would do anything for those people. In the U.S., people have all kinds of places to go [with their needs]. Down there they only had Father Rother." When twins María and Mercedes were born in the village, the whole Coo family visited the rectory each evening to get bottles, formula, nutritional supplements, and extra food. "They would come in and kiss his hand and visit with him," Frankie remembered. Watching Father Stanley make his way on foot around the village — or down the church aisle — was very much "like the stories in the Bible about Jesus," with people trying to touch him, and a trail of giggling children following him and grabbing his hands.

In a 1977 newspaper interview, Father Stanley described his pastoral work at the mission — and his love for the Tz'utujil people:

> Dealing with the cultural differences that exist within the parish between the Ladinos and the Tz'utujil people is the most difficult problem I have to deal with.... I speak the Tz'utujil language and because I have close relationships among the Tz'utujil, there is a kind of jealousy in some of the Ladinos. In the eyes of some people, I'm identified more with the Tz'utujil and they think I prefer the Tz'utujil to the Ladinos. I probably do because I feel more accepted by the Tz'utujil.[19]

One of Father Thomas Boyer's fondest memories about Santiago Atitlán was celebrating Mass with Father Stanley. "It wasn't pious. It was deeply reverent, it was peaceful … it was the true breaking of the bread of the Body of Christ," explained Father Boyer, who was ordained five years after Father Stanley.

"I loved the way he said Mass," agreed Sister Marita. "I heard him give a sermon once in Okarche that impressed me. He was so strong on the theme of the Mystical Body of Christ, that we are all one in Christ … he did such a good job, even though he did all of a sudden go off into Spanish! He just laughed and came back to English," she remembered, laughing.

Father Stanley celebrated every Mass "as though it was very personal, the most important Mass of his life," agreed Frankie Williams, who was Methodist. "For outsiders like me, it was a pleasure to watch the reverence, compared to a rote recitation of the prayers." In the same slow, deliberate, thoughtful way that he spoke, Father Stanley celebrated the Eucharist, "with deliberate reverence and attention." Frankie remembered being with Father Stanley as he celebrated Mass for two people and for 3,000 people — "always with feeling and adoration and celebration. He never once hurried through one.... I always felt attending Mass down [in Santiago Atitlán] was more reverent than here. He was an inspirational person when you saw him with those people." With him, "everything was done in a very gentle, quiet manner."

The Gift of Humor

Although Father Stanley once told her that he was better one-on-one, Frankie remembered him being charming in a crowd. "He had a beautiful laugh, a great sense of humor ... and he could tell stories on himself and just sort of chuckle." Once during a homily, with a beautiful young woman in front of him, Father Stanley got the Spanish word for house [*casa*] confused with the Spanish word for bed [*cama*], and ended up making the statement, "Christ said, come into my bed." Whether embarrassed by the event — or by how easily Father Stanley was embarrassed as a new missionary priest — Frankie Williams remembered laughing with Father Stanley years later about his simple but significant mistake.

Father Stanley had an "infectious laughter," remembered his fifth-grade teacher, Sister Clarissa Tenbrink. "His laughter rang so true. And he had beautiful eyes and a beautiful smile; you couldn't help but smile back." After teaching him in Okarche, Sister Clarissa kept up a friendship with Father Stanley through the years by phone, letters, and even a one-week visit to Guatemala. "He was one of the few people, even as a child, I could look into his eyes and see goodness." Father Stanley had a tremendous sense of humor, she said, which he expressed in his teasing. His letters to her often would include a new joke.

After dropping her off at the Guatemala City airport, Sister Clarissa recalled, Father Stanley and co-worker Sister Johanna began the drive back to Santiago Atitlán, but were blocked by a mudslide that closed the road. In Father Stanley's next letter to Sister Clarissa, he described a funny story about the event, one that he was very proud of retelling. Father Stanley looked at Sister Johanna, with whom he had a difficult working relationship, and said to her: "Johanna, whether you like it or not, you're going to have to sleep with me tonight."

One of the ways that Father Stanley expressed his humor was by playing pranks on his friends — much as he did growing up with his siblings. When his friend Don Moore came to visit him in Guatemala, for example, Father Don walked out of the plane and Father Stanley was nowhere to be seen. Father Don remembered going through all the confusion of immigration and customs in a foreign language — and still, there was no sign of his friend. It wasn't until Father Don, reluctantly, had a porter pick up his luggage, to take him to a taxi, that he heard Father Stanley's laugh nearby. "He was a great prankster," Father Don said, smiling. "When he was up to something mischievous, he had a twinkle in his eye."

Perhaps it was because they were able to easily laugh together, but Frankie was not daunted by what some people described as Father Stanley's temper. "I found that he could be pretty grumpy and non-communicative," Frankie described, adding that she and fellow volunteer Bertha Sánchez would simply give him space when that happened and declare, "This is bear day."

"He had difficulty in communication," explained Bertha, who lived in the rectory compound during her five years as a clinic nurse at Santiago Atitlán. "I think he found it difficult to say what he was thinking." Yet ultimately, "if many people were frightened of him by his non-smiling demeanor, they knew they could go to him for help," and the situations he found himself in as a missionary often brought out his good sense of humor. Bertha recalled a visit to one of the fincas for Mass. "The chapel was very narrow, and the women sling their babies over their backs. A two- or three-year-old child was toddling around near the altar. When the kid grabbed the sombrero of a man and bothered him, a woman displayed her breast and teased the child to her breast for nursing.... Stan had a hard time not laughing."

Dr. John Emrich, who volunteered at the clinic over eight years, described those moments this way: "Always a stern face, but always helped ... he was a very generous man." As his co-worker David Iven noted, "I don't recall him ever having a temper tantrum. My recollection of Stan is he would just clam up and go to his room." If after reflection, however, Stanley decided that what he had done or said was wrong or improper, he would come back and try to make it right, apologize — whether to a volunteer co-worker or a parishioner.

"He had a temper and he knew it," remarked Sister Charlotte Rohr, who served in Santiago Atitlán for three years and returned as a volunteer for four more summers. "It exploded one time when I came back from the city. I had two visitors with me. There had been problems with the Bronco. When I got home, we were late. When I told Stan he got so mad. Instead of sympathizing with us he got mad about that old car."

The following Saturday when Sister Charlotte and Father Stanley went on a visit to one of the coffee fincas, he took the opportunity to discuss with her his difficulty. He asked her, "How do you control your temper?" Her advice: Keep still and say a prayer. Father Stanley must have taken the advice to heart, and to prayer. Weeks later he asked Sister Charlotte if she had noticed an improvement, to which she could honestly say that she had.

One story of Father Stanley's temperament that made the rounds and provoked great laughter among fellow missionaries throughout the Santiago Atitlán region involved hippies. Apparently, during the 1970s, American hippies found their way to the resort town of Panajachel, across the lake from Santiago Atitlán — and some hippies made their way by boat to the village, and to the parish mission. As the story goes, a hippie wandered into the rectory one day and apparently found an empty bed where he proceeded to take a nap. When Father Stanley found him, he woke up the longhaired man and told him that it was time for him to leave. But the hippie, perhaps in a haze of drugs, proceeded to argue with Father Stanley, saying that "as an American" he had a right to use the bed — and that brought any further discussion to an end. Father Stanley grabbed the man, dragged him out of the rectory, and flung him down the stone steps and into the church plaza. And the story lived on in infamy!

If hippies and their arrogance brought out Father Stanley's edginess, it was the smallest and the neediest near him that brought out a deep well of patience.

In January 1976, Sololá's Bishop Angélico Melotto sent a freshly ordained Father Adán García to serve as Father Stanley's assistant, and the new, 25-year-old energetic priest was immediately given the satellite parish of Cerro de Oro as part of his duties. A native of nearby San Lucas Tolimán, Father Adán was a Ladino and well acquainted with the complicated dynamics of ministering in that region — and Father Stanley readily liked him.

The Great Earthquake of 1976

At 3 a.m. on Wednesday, February 4, 1976, a massive earthquake startled and woke Father Stanley. Like California, Guatemala is known as "earthquake country." Being used to dozens of tremors a year, Father Stanley didn't realize at first the magnitude of what had just happened. That first massive tremor, centered near the town of Los Amates, had a magnitude of 7.5. Located six miles under the Earth's surface and 120 miles northwest of Guatemala City, sleeping residents of the capital city were crushed and killed when their adobe homes collapsed on top of them. In a matter of minutes, about one-third of that city was destroyed.

The quake was the result of an enormous clash between the Caribbean and North American plates on Guatemala's Motagua Fault. Although efforts to rescue the thousands of people buried beneath the rubble began immediately, the number of people that could not be saved was immense. The roads and bridges leading to Guatemala City had been extensively damaged — and many landslides continued to occur, making it extremely difficult to get help to the city. Food and water supplies were severely reduced. Some of the areas were without electricity and communication for days, even weeks.

In the Santiago Atitlán region, the catastrophic earthquake fractured the Lake Atitlán bed, causing subsurface drainage from the lake and allowing the water level to drop two meters within one month. The village of Santiago Atitlán, however, was almost completely spared. Even its ancient church suffered only minimal damage: a few pieces of masonry fell from old cracks in the bell tower, and one large statue inside the church toppled from its ledge. But word quickly arrived that only 10 miles away there was serious devastation, with many dead and injured at the hamlet of Agua Escondido. The main earthquake shock was followed by thousands of strong aftershocks for an entire week, terrorizing the survivors — and causing additional loss of life and damage.

Father Stanley, along with two doctors and two nurses from the mission's Project Concern, immediately prepared to offer assistance, but they had to wait three full days for the road to San Lucas to reopen. When they were finally able to reach the outlying areas affected by the giant quake, their efforts concentrated on the city of Patzun, only 18 air miles away — but four hours distant because of the condition of the roads. Father Stanley described the team's efforts: "We worked for three days with the local emergency committee, attending the injured, moving food and medical supplies, bringing patients out [of] the remote rural areas to medical facilities for treatment. At noon on Tuesday we found and carried out a woman that had a fractured pelvis and shoulder." About 1,000 people died in Patzun.

Father Stanley described the outpouring of help by the people of Santiago Atitlán as "tremendous." When an appeal was made for food to feed the victims, the people of the town responded with so many tortillas, boiled eggs, and canned juices that some had to be left behind for later delivery. Eventually four tons of corn and beans as well as some cash were given to the relief effort.

Father Adán García was impressed by Father Stanley's determination and actions during the rescue efforts. "He was the only one strong enough and brave enough to go into the ravines where the poor people lived," he recalled. Father Stanley filled the pickup with all kinds of equipment from the Santiago Atitlán hospital. The streets were destroyed. "The people were in the valleys and the donkeys couldn't get there. Helicopters couldn't land. He was so strong, he brought injured people on his own shoulders up the slopes … like climbing a mountain."

Eighteen miles away, in the town of Chimaltenango, Sister Rosa Valentina Xinico Sipac described that first night of terror for her community of Carmelite Missionaries: "It was like a dream, very early in the morning. I felt that God still wanted me to live." Four sisters in her room died instantly, while two others were covered in debris but lived. Sister Rosa Valentina remembered that she "got up, jumped out and everything collapsed … only one house in the pueblo was standing afterward … the sisters were in uncontrollable grief."

American missionary Sister Trinitas Keltgen also remembered Father Stanley's efforts during those terrible days at Patzun: "The earthquake destroyed our whole town…. One morning I was crawling out of the tent and there stood Stan. Just seeing him was a real sign of hope. He said, 'Trini, I'm sorry,' and he gave me a big hug.... We walked downtown and he helped the priest give Communion" outside the flattened church.

Back in Santiago Atitlán, Father Stanley and the medical staff offered the hospital facilities in their village for some of the wounded. U.S. Army helicopters transported the injured from remote areas there, including 15 persons from Patzun. "[Father] Stan put up visiting doctors at the mission," recalled nurse Bertha Sánchez. "It was his way of thanking the doctors and their team [for their efforts after the earthquake]." A few weeks after the big quake, another relief group from Santiago Atitlán made its way to Santa Apolonia, an isolated village and the site of a mission staffed by American priests. The place had been devastated, but the injured had been treated by the time the crew from Santiago Atitlán arrived.

When the final tally was put together, the numbers related to the 1976 earthquake were catastrophic. Over 26,000 people were dead, and more than 80,000 were injured. Approximately 258,000 houses had been destroyed, leaving about 1.2 million people homeless. Sixteen of the 22 political divisions in the country were affected. Because 40 percent of the national hospital infrastructure had been destroyed and other health facilities suffered substantial damage, the U.S. Air Force continued to assist by airlifting food and medicine into the area for weeks. With all the available hospitals filled beyond capacity, the United States military also set up a field hospital in Chimaltenango. The number of deceased in Guatemala overwhelmed the authorities so much that communal gravesites were established.

Following the earthquake, Bishop Melotto needed a dependable person to coordinate the relief work in the Diocese of Sololá, where half of all the churches had been destroyed. The bishop chose Father Adán. "At least I had an assistant for awhile.... He shows up at Cerro de Oro most Sundays for Mass and then is gone again," Father Stanley wrote to his Oklahoma friend Father Marvin Leven in June 1976. "Maybe it is good for me. Before, there was always someone else who was available for anointings, blessing of the dead and daily Mass — now I have to be available. I find myself being around the rectory more and less out working some place."

The same month Stanley matter-of-factly reported to Sister Marita, "I have two Masses every Saturday and two fincas (involving long, difficult mountain drives) and then three on Sunday in Atitlán. Easter Sunday I had five Masses." A year later Father Stanley wrote to Sister Marita: "My associate is still working nine-tenths of his time out of the parish.... It might just be that I'll get the new Indian priest to be ordained late this fall and Adán will go somewhere else. I'll have to put a bug in the bishop's ear. I like Adán, but I don't think he could settle down here and this is too close to San Lucas and his home." Father Adán remained an associate to Father Stanley for four years.

Meanwhile, back in the United Sates, Bishop Charles A. Salatka, from the Diocese of Marquette, Michigan, was installed as archbishop of Oklahoma City on December 15, 1977. By his own admission, Archbishop Salatka didn't know much about the Guatemala mission, but he understood *why* it was there. "I certainly agreed with the request.... I became more and more aware of what kind of mission it was, one of those things that grows on you," Archbishop Salatka remembered years later. "Father Stanley was very, very aware of the condition of his people, and there was no question he came to serve ... his whole self was there. He was there for the right reasons. His life was enough for the people to take him into their hearts.... [He was] a sincere, full-hearted priest."

Where Two or More Are Gathered

Like MICATOKLA, many of the missions in the highlands of Guatemala had started out with a large team of missionaries — and over the years dwindled down to one priest. The remaining men shared one important criteria in common: most of them were diocesan priests, prepared by their training to work in parishes throughout the United States but diverted to Guatemala by the plea of Pope John XXIII to help the Church in Latin America. Veteran Maryknoll missionary Father Jim Curtin recognized this unique situation and generously agreed to direct a monthly support group that would give them encouragement and spiritual reinforcement. And although Father Curtin served as the leader, he did not inhibit others from contributing.

"We all had the same problem, isolation," explained Father James Hazelton of the Diocese of Helena, Montana. All of the missionaries served predominantly indigenous populations; people whom they loved, but also people whose customs and approach to life would always remain somewhat foreign to outsiders.

Recalling those years, all members of the support group noted how much they looked forward each month to the 24-hour break from their regular mission routine. They came together about noon the first day, spent time talking, lounging about the pool, eating, and praying. On the morning of the second day they celebrated Mass together.

Father Ron Burke of San Francisco described the more serious moments of the group meetings as a "review of life." The process was for each of them, one by one and without rushing, to present an incident or item in his life for review, seeking others' guidance and direction in better discerning the will of God. Father Jim McGreevy of the Diocese of Spokane remembered Father Stanley with a definitive and insightful simple sentence: "Stan was good to people whom other people avoided."

Veteran social justice activist Father Burke recalled Father Stanley as a "quiet, stoic, gentle" man of great convictions — with whom he disagreed strongly about how much American priests should be raising their voices for social justice in Guatemala. Father Stanley held that, as foreigners, Americans should let the local people be the ones who voiced any protests. Yet "no sooner had he said that, than he began to speak out," Father Burke noted. But Father Stanley "wasn't there just for social ministry, which was a real danger for a lot of priests," emphasized Father David Vavasseur of the Diocese of Baton Rouge. "I got a lot of inspiration from him."

"He was rugged physically, always talked about back on the farm, very friendly. Children felt an affinity for him. He was a pleasure to be around ... so simple. He didn't put on airs," Father Vavasseur said. "He was solid as a rock. We admired him. He was definitely a man of prayer ... and was willing to share his experiences in the group." Like Father Stanley, Father Vavasseur faced immense obstacles at the Santa Apolonia mission, where he served, and the priests' support group provided both spiritual nourishment and productive exchanges of ideas. "We tried to keep each other honest."

If Father Stanley had a fault in his perspective on mission work, it was a naïveté regarding how the political situation affected it — and the people involved, explained Benedictine Father Patrick Greene, who met Father Stanley at the Maryknoll House in Guatemala City and was in close contact with him as their situation became more dangerous. "Stan may have been a little naïve … a few of the people, they knew he was so good, and took advantage of him," he added. "I think he could not really believe that some of these wonderful people around here were involved with the guerrillas."

Build My Church

Father Stanley being the builder that he was, it is not a big surprise to find out that one of his significant interests was updating and taking care of the 400-year-old church building where he celebrated Mass every week. Aware that the sensibility of the Tz'utujil involved the need to visibly express and experience the sacred, Father Stanley began working on one project after another to bring beauty, theology, and relatability to the Iglesia Parroquial Santiago Apóstol. A severe earthquake in 1960 had heavily damaged the roof, the bell tower, and several of the altarpieces and decorations.

After ordering stained-glass windows from a firm in Mexico City through the mission's funds, Father Stanley made the long drive north to pick them up and transport them himself to Santiago Atitlán. He, of course, also led the installation process, a tricky, tedious, and long-term project — working on them when he had spare hours. In a 1975 year-end letter he wrote, "The stained glass windows that I started installing two years ago are still not finished. But this church has stood for over 400 years and will likely stand for several hundred more."

After completing the more serious structural repairs, Father Stanley turned his attention to the three carved wooden altarpieces. The two side altars required minimal work — reinforcing the wood frames that had warped and cracked over the centuries and reattaching some of the fallen pieces. But the massive main altarpiece was a different story. Not only had it suffered the most damage in the 1960 earthquake, but for decades, perhaps even centuries, an altar had stood in front of — and hiding — an ancient, ornate, wooden retableau (retablo) that soars some 18 to 20 feet high. And the pieces that the earthquake caused to fall or crack had been removed from the church and left stacked with other broken fragments, divided in various storage rooms in the parish complex. With his keen artist eye — and perhaps with memories of the vivid and meaningful images at his Okarche home church — Father Stanley envisioned updating and restoring the wood featuring new carvings of Tz'utujil figures at work and at prayer.

He began by securing two local expert woodcarvers — brothers Diego and Nicolás Chávez — discussing in detail how to remove the ancient grime, restore the pieces, and incorporate traditional Tz'utujil Mayan tradition. Like texts and artifacts, the wooden altarpiece for the Mayans is considered a living thing endowed with a *k'u'x* (heart), which was placed there by the ancestors, for the Tz'utujil community. This meant that Father Stanley's efforts to restore and repair the wood altarpiece carried spiritually important and healing significance for his parishioners.

"The retableau or altar background in the church will be mostly finished for Christmas. That is really good news," Father Stanley wrote at Christmas 1979. "Since there were many parts and columns of old altar pieces stacked in the corner of the church, we got the idea of putting up a big retableau where they apparently had one before. It will end up being about half new and half old, but an interesting mosaic of woods."

Also in his sphere of dreams, Father Stanley imagined various scenarios for creating a meeting place separate from the church that could accommodate a large number of people, not a small objective for a parish made up of 25,000 parishioners. When a crazy offer came their way — purchasing the steel frame of a would-be church that was already erected but no longer wanted — Father Stanley jumped at the idea. For a bargain $8,000, Father Stanley and his crew of volunteers took down the erected steel frame, and proceeded to transport it over many miles and narrow twisting roads to Santiago Atitlán. Meanwhile, his associate Father Adán García, through his Caritas connections, appealed to the German bishops for a donation of $30,000 to complete the task of setting up the hall — and received $20,000 in response.

On Father Stanley's list of priorities, completing the language project that his mentor and friend Father Ramon Carlin had begun ranked very high. Even though the budget was tight and regularly diminishing, Father Stanley continued to support the work of translating Scripture and everyday prayers into Tz'utujil being carried out by Antonio Tzina Ratzan and Juan Mendoza. The complete three-year liturgical cycle for Sunday Masses was completed first, followed by other texts used in Sunday worship. By the late 1970s, the two translators had produced a 200-page Spanish-Tz'utujil prayer book for Santiago Atitlán — and they were far along in the task of translating the entire New Testament for their people. Being carried out at the same time, classes were organized to teach the Tz'utujil people how to read and write their own language — for the first time in known Mayan history.

Father Stanley still carried in his heart the same love for liturgical and classical music that led him to become a member of the Schola Cantorum during his seminary years — and to attend concerts of the Oklahoma City Symphony Orchestra as a newly ordained priest. Mission volunteers frequently recalled how much Father Stanley loved to sit in his chair at the end of a long day, reading, and listening to music, such as recordings of the Weston Choral Society. So when a college choral group from Huntsville, Alabama, requested permission to perform in the historic Santiago Atitlán church, Father Stanley immediately agreed. The singers performed before a packed crowd in a church that fits 2,000-plus — and the audience loved the music, especially the accompanying stringed instruments.

One day a couple came to see Father Stanley with a tiny four-pound baby in their arms. They explained that the woman had given birth to twins, but the family could not afford to take care of both of them, so they gave Father Stanley a small bundle named María — whom he received without hesitation. "Padre Francisco got up in the middle of the night to fix her formula," Aurea Albiso Merida recalled. "He changed her diapers, took care of her." Older people and children were his "specialty," Aurea emphasized, but when the political situation became volatile in the late 1970s, even more parents dropped by seeking help from their pastor. "A lot of people would bring babies to Padre Francisco. He would find mothers for them."

Since powder formula had been banned from the village by Project Concern's medical staff — out of their concern that the formula would be mixed with polluted water — Father Stanley raced away to purchase the closest liquid formula available for baby María. Father Stanley's aunt, Sister Bridget Smith, happened to be visiting the mission at that time and became baby María's day nurse. At night, nurse Bertha Sánchez cared for the baby. This continued for several weeks, as baby María's weight increased from four to six pounds.

When former priest Jude Pansini and his wife arrived in July 1977 to join in the celebration of the town's Fiesta in honor of their patron St. James, Father Stanley approached the couple with an unexpected request involving baby María. And the Pansinis said yes, agreeing to adopt the baby girl.

Sister Marita emphasized, "Among the poor is where I really saw why he wanted to work there. Because he was really helping … he was doing what he had to do, and it all made sense," explaining what a difference it made for her to watch Father Stanley among the Tz'utujil. "It was the greatest blessing seeing him in action. He was so himself there. I can't tell you how much of that he did *not* show when he came home," she said, and then paused.

"When I was there, we did have time to talk in the evenings, about what he had done during the day. But we never had to say a whole lot to know how we felt." When she pictures her big brother in her mind today, Sister Marita said she loves seeing him standing on the porch, looking out over the village, and smoking his pipe. But her favorite image is of him "walking down the aisle out of church, because he's touching every person as he comes out ... and the kids are running to him, and he's patting him or her on the head.... That was his home. Those were his people."

Watching Storms Building from a Distance

Growing up in a farm family in Oklahoma, Stanley Rother must have learned at an early age to read the signs in the sky that indicate a major storm is brewing. Long before the crash of lightning and the unrelenting winds that come sweeping down the plain, a farmer learns to notice what others cannot see. The subtle shift in pressure, the shift in wind direction, the feeling in the air — all commanding, pay attention!

An intense and terrifying man-made storm was already brewing over Central America in the late 1970s, and its deadly black clouds had expanded into Guatemala, wreaking havoc in Guatemala City and the Atlantic side of the country. Father Stanley took note. In a long letter to his seminary friend Harry Flynn, then rector of Mount St. Mary's Seminary in Emmitsburg, Maryland, he wrote:

My note in January [1978] for the persecuted Church in Latinamerica certainly has rung true here in Guatemala. At the end of May there was a massacre in the Northern part of the Country and about 115 men, women and children died. Then June 30th, there was an activist priest [Guatemalan] cut down by submachine gun fire just outside Guatemala City. Over the past few years there have been numerous catechists killed in various parts of the Country. Just last week another one was cut down who was helping organize a union among miners. He had worked with the Maryknoll Fathers before that as a teacher. It is almost certain that the Maryknoll priest who died in the Fall of '76 had his plane sabotaged. Other parts of Latinamerica are worse.

Although the violence and upheaval was for a while kept away from the Lake Atitlán region, the guerrillas were slowly extending west into the Pacific highland mountains — and the government responded immediately. The storm that seemed for so long to be taking place far away from the Lake Atitlán region suddenly and violently descended upon the indigenous Mayans, who were already experiencing hardship and shocking poverty.

In an end-of-the-year mission report, in 1978, Father Stanley described his disgust at the treatment of the indigenous people of Guatemala:

On the Pacific Coast here in Guatemala, there are hundreds of plantations that produce cotton, sugar cane, coffee and beef for export. This land is owned by relatively few people. But there are over one million Guatemalans who are landless peasants. They would like to be able to feed themselves instead of sending sugar, cotton and beef to compete with the American farmer. The country here needs exports, but at the expense of the very people that provide the basis for the ever increasing tourist trade? Several years ago a present high government official suggested that all Indian males be sterilized to get rid of the "Indian Problem." Their wives would be impregnated by the non-Indians to "improve" the race with Spanish blood. But then this would ruin the "native" or "primitive" aspect of the lure of tourism. Therefore ... Man's inhumanity to man!

In a May 1979 letter to Sister Marita, Father Stanley confessed that "an anonymous hate sheet or vomit sheet, like someone said, made its debut a few Sundays ago. The mayor, the school director, teachers, and anybody of importance in town made the list. I was number 8 and [Father] Adán number 9. It was interesting to see just how much information they had, some of it misjudged, half-truths, and just outright lies."

"The political situation here is really sad," he continued. "Guatemala is systematically doing away with all liberal[s] or even moderates in government, [as well as] the labor leaders and apparently there are lots of kidnappings that never get in the papers. There are something like 15 bodies that show up every day in the country and show signs of torture and then shot." Lastly, Father Stanley revealed to Sister Marita that his associate, Father Adán, had recently received two threatening letters and is "running scared." One of Father Adán's priest friends had experienced two attempted kidnappings. About himself, he wrote:

> I haven't received any threats as such, but if anything happens that is the way it's supposed to be. I don't intend to run from danger, but at the same time I don't intend to unnecessarily put myself into danger. I want to live like anyone else. What I have told you here is just for you, not to say any of this to the folks.... We just need the help of God to do our work well and to be able to take it if the time comes that we are asked to suffer for Him.

Nine months later, Father Stanley wrote a long letter to Sister Marita, wherein he admitted:

> The political situation here and elsewhere in the world is something else. There were killings by the police and army in the Spanish Embassy in Guatemala [City]. On the Coast here, fields are being burned, strikes at sugar mills, buildings and equipment on the fincas being destroyed, even trucks loaded with cotton bales being stopped and burned. All traffic is stopped and searched at strategic points. Everyone blames everyone else and the tension builds, more killings, repression. Don't know when it will all stop. It will get worse before it gets better.

In May 1980, Father Stanley was approached by a group of sisters about coming to work at the Santiago Apóstol parish. What made the Carmelites of St. Teresa unique was that the community consisted almost completely of professed Indian sisters from different Mayan groups — something unheard of at the time. Since encouraging and supporting Mayan vocations was important to Father Stanley, he was quite pleased when the arrangement materialized. The sisters would work at the parish in the areas of literacy, catechism, and liturgical music, as well as working directly with the girls, the women, and the sick of the community.

That same month, Father Stanley went home to Oklahoma to celebrate his sister's 25th anniversary as a member of the Adorers of the Blood of Christ sisters, and to have a short vacation with his family. The 45-year-old pastor returned to Santiago Atitlán a month later, marking the beginning of the most challenging year of his life.

CHAPTER 6

He Died an Atiteco

In January of 1980, Bishop Angélico Melotto assigned Father Pedro Bocel, a full-blooded Cakchiquel Indian, to serve as Father Stanley Rother's associate pastor at Santiago Atitlán and its outpost missions. In his 1979-1980 Financial Summary submitted to the mission's two sponsoring dioceses in Oklahoma, Father Stanley the administrator notes two items of special interest to him. "The retableau [his long-term project to beautify the church] is now finished in the Church and the expenses there will be much less this year." And "The Sisters [Carmelite Missionaries of St. Teresa] accepted my counter proposal of $400 per month to work here in the parish. Since this is not included in the budget, I would like to ask for $100 a month as your 'modest' increase for the services of the Sisters. They will start here in September."

First Signs of Danger

Meanwhile, the situation throughout Guatemala continued to worsen: massacres by the Guatemalan army; killings instigated by a number of different guerrilla groups, each with its own agenda; death squads operating with silent government approval. In the Sololá region, the death squad most active was called Mano Blanca — but there was nothing white and innocent about them. In June 1980, members of the guerrilla group ORPA (Organization of the People at Arms) marched into Santiago Atitlán and occupied the town square for a few hours. People gathered in the plaza in front of the parish church and heard members of ORPA criticize Guatemala's president, General Fernando Romeo Lucas García, condemning his government on a number of things, but especially for its mistreatment of its own people. When their open-air meeting concluded, the uninvited visitors left the town peacefully.

It may not seem like much, but this event became the match that lighted the government's attention on Santiago Atitlán and the Sololá region.

That same month, the bishops of Guatemala issued a pastoral letter denouncing "the persecution in which the Church finds itself," including the torture and killing of catechists, priests, and other Christians:

> The acts of violence among us have taken on unimaginable forms: there are murders, kidnappings, torture and even vicious desecrations of the victims' bodies.... We pastoral agents are continually watched, our sermons are taped, and our every activity is checked. In a country basically Catholic, three priests have recently been murdered and another kidnapped. Several other priests and religious are threatened with death, and others have been expelled from the country. For us there is special significance in the circumstances surrounding

the violent death of Father José María Gran Ciera, S.H.M., pastor of Chajul, who was shot in the back as he returned home by horseback after having gone to minister to the numerous members of his parish in the remote villages, accompanied only by his sacristan, Mr. Domingo Bats, also murdered.

A part of this religious persecution is the campaign of discredit and slander aimed at certain bishops, priests and religious, a campaign that tends to create a climate of distrust in the body of the faithful toward the legitimate pastors.... The very priests who have offered their lives as martyrs for Christ, in preaching the Gospel, have been afterwards the object of insidious calumnies meant to blacken their obvious Christian witness.

In a letter to his friend and mission volunteer Frankie Williams, Father Stanley described what he encountered on his return to Guatemala:

[O]verhead is a meeting of campesinos looking for self-protection, the men of the Church are painting the porch blue, it is trying to rain, tourists are coming into the Church to look and then go again, the morning's paper said that someone tried to kill the alcalde [mayor] of Escuintla yesterday, another University professor was killed, various unidentified and tortured bodies showed up, etc. And so goes life in Guatemala. It is really something to be living in the midst of all this. There was another priest killed to the North of us in Quiche while

I was gone. That makes three since the first of May. One was kidnapped, presumed dead. And what do we do about all this? What can we do, but do our work, keep our heads down, preach the gospel of love and non-violence, etc. We can show people the way, but if they are hell bent on a collision course with the powers that be, then there is little that my preaching will change if at all…. Now don't be too preoccupied, nothing is going to happen. God will take care of His own, if we are in that group nothing will happen that isn't supposed to. It is all part of His great plan.

Not surprisingly, once the government heard about the impromptu rally held in June by the guerrillas at the town plaza, it sent its army. The first to arrive were members of the Guatemalan army on motorcycles, and they began questioning individual Tz'utujil about the event, and more: Who was there? Who in the crowd applauded? Who works at the radio station? What about the people with the church?

In the midst of that ominous scenario, the Santiago parish and its priests, and a legion of catechists, all combined forces to prepare hundreds of candidates for the sacraments of initiation — First Holy Communion, Penance, and Confirmation — to be received during the 1980 village Fiesta of St. James. In addition, there was a larger than usual group of couples readying for marriage. Village tradition mandated that the sacraments always take place as part of the Fiesta on July 25 — the major feast celebrating the parish and the town, both named after St. James the Apostle. The Fiesta began early and went on long into the evening, always including carnival games and rides in the plaza, as well as elaborate processions carrying the church statues dressed in special garments, especially St. James.

Summer in Santiago Atitlán also meant longer visits from regular volunteers from the United States, including Father Stanley's good friend Father Marvin Leven, whose tradition was to spend his personal vacation helping at the mission for two or three weeks at a time.

In the final six years of Father Stanley's life, Father Leven was the Oklahoma priest closest to him. "There were times when I needed to talk to someone who would listen," Father Leven said later. "[Those visits were] a good time of retreat." Father Stanley felt the same way: "I sure appreciated your coming down here with me and staying as long as you did. I believe it did both of us good," he once wrote. And after another visit: "You really don't know how much good your visit was for all of us. We hope it was a good time for you too, and that you went back refreshed."

In the months of August and September of 1980, Father Stanley became aware of an increasing number of strangers in Santiago Atitlán. His parishioners informed him that the visitors were engaging many locals in conversation, asking specific questions related to the parish: the priests, the catechists, the heads of cooperatives, the radio station, and other leaders of the village. This news spread quickly among the Tz'utujil and the Ladinos alike. A number of the more prominent Tz'utujil began to plan their escape, quietly boarding buses for Guatemala City, making their way by launch across the lake to Panajachel, or simply fading into the mountains to hide.

Meanwhile, Father Stanley reinforced the security at the mission compound, securing doors and gates. For the first time in the history of the MICATOKLA mission, the front door to the rectory was kept locked at all times. And its pastor moved his sleeping quarters. "I sleep elsewhere now where the walls are rock instead of wood," he wrote to a friend. In his 13 years at the mission, Father Stan had always slept on the second floor, in a bedroom facing the church plaza. After he heard about attacks using hand grenades that shattered wooden walls, he quietly moved downstairs to what had become a kind of living room, where Father Stanley used a pullout sofa as his bed.

On his walks around town and to and from the radio station, Father Pedro Bocel started experiencing threatening situations where he realized that he was being followed. One morning, for example, after doing the radio broadcast at 6 a.m., Father Pedro saw three men in a dark car waiting for him on the road. "I consider it a miracle," he recalled later. "I walked right in front of them, and they didn't recognize me." But as soon as they realized their mistake, they started stalking him. Father Pedro's immediate instinct was to go into a store to hide, watching the car drive back and forth on the street. He remained there until a friend came to confirm that the street was clear. These experiences not only spooked Father Pedro, but they also worried Father Stanley. He decided it was time to write his superior, Oklahoma City's Archbishop Charles Salatka, describing the haunting reality they were facing in Santiago Atitlán. The letter is dated September 22, 1980.

"Since the first of May, 1980, there have been four priests killed here in the Country. All have been foreigners, but none have been from the States," Father Stan began. Continuing, he wrote:

> The Diocese of Quiche, to the North of Sololá, has been abandoned completely. The Bishop even left the Diocese. Two priests were killed, catechists, lay people, etc. were killed and the rest of the priests left to stay alive. The repression continues there and at one place there were about 60 men of the Church lined up by the wall and they killed every fourth person.
>
> The country here is in rebellion and the government is taking it out on the Church. The low wages that are paid, the very few who are excessively rich, the bad distribution of land — these are some of the reasons for the widespread discontent. The Church seems to be the only force that is trying to do something [about] the situation, and therefore the government is after us. There are some that say the Diocese of Sololá, where this mission is, is the next area on the list for persecution. In one parish of the Diocese that is served by a priest from Spokane, he can only enter once in a while, and at that unannounced. A Christian Brother in the same area was sent back to Spain by the Bishop for an extended vacation. Another priest from Houston that works in the area too was told last week by the Bishop to leave for a rest. Both were on the move all the time because they knew that they were being controlled and in danger.

Here in Atitlán, we are very cautious. The army was here in force during the fiesta the latter part of July, dressed in camouflage fatigues and carrying submachine guns. They didn't do anything but put everyone on edge, walking around in groups of three or four, standing on the corners watching everything. Since then we have had strangers in town, asking questions about the priests, this catechist or that one, where they live, who is in charge of the Cooperative, who are the leaders, etc. Because of this intimidation, several of the leaders of the different organizations are out of town or in hiding. It has changed our style of life here in the rectory too....

I am aware that some of our younger catechists are working with those that are preparing for a revolution. They are young men that are becoming more and more conscientious about their situation and are convinced that the only option for them is revolt. The more unrest and action against the government, the more that the government is pushing repression. There was a so-called popular concentration in Guatemala City the 7th of September, where teachers, government employees etc. were obliged to attend in order to keep their jobs. The President [Fernando Romeo Lucas García] gave a speech where he laid aside the prepared text and spoke from the cuff. I haven't seen the official text, but one remark made was that he wanted to expel all those religious who were catechizing the people. Then he asked the people there if he should do that, and they applauded. So we don't know just what to expect now.

The reality is that we are in danger. But we don't know when or what form the government will use to further repress the Church. For a month or so now, all classes and group meetings have been canceled. We are working in smaller groups. My associate and myself are seen less in the street, and almost never leave the rectory at night. The tactic of the government has been to kidnap those they think are leaders, torture them and then kill them....

If I should be told to leave here, it would be almost impossible for Father Pedro Bocel to continue here alone. Being a Guatemalan and an Indian, it is more probable that he will be dispatched first. That is the reason that I am wanting to get him a visa. I do not intend to leave him here to be killed if I have to leave, or if we see that he is in imminent danger, I want to get him out of the Country. He was just ordained in January and I feel he should not have to be sacrificed so early in his ministry. He could easily work in a Mexican-American area of the Archdiocese and then return here after the danger has subsided. I don't feel that you would deny him that chance to escape from almost certain death here if things continue to evolve as they have been. I am not in as much danger as he is, because I am a foreigner and I hope they will give me a chance of leaving if they want me out. They haven't killed an American priest yet.

Given the situation, I am not ready to leave here just yet. There is a chance the Government will back off. If I get a direct threat or am told to leave, then I will go. But if it is my destiny that I should give my life here, then so be it. Like the priest in the neighboring parish said to me, "I like martyrs, but just to read about them." I don't want to desert these people, and that is what will be said, even after all these years. There is still a lot of good that can be done under the circumstances.

Archbishop, I hope you understand now our situation and why I am interested in getting a visa for Fr. Pedro. Pray for us that we may continue to serve as best we can in the reality where we find ourselves.

The Violence Reaches Lake Atitlán

The first sound they heard was the low humming rumble of military trucks as they shifted gears, a long line of them, each truck weighed down by groups of soldiers and their equipment. The convoy snaked its way through the winding road between San Lucas and Santiago Atitlán, and finally through the narrow streets of the village. The troops stopped on the outskirts of Santiago Atitlán at Panabaj canton, setting encampment on October 21, 1980 — and trespassing into part of the finca owned and run by the parish.

"There were army guys on motorcycles snooping around and asking questions, just sort of terrorizing," recalled Project Concern's Dr. John Emrich. "I remember the army coming in and setting up by the hospital. One by one, they picked off people." The army blocked some of the streets and military plainclothes men walked the town, making their presence known.

At midnight, on October 23, a group of five well-dressed men forced their way into the small hut of Gaspar Culan Yataz and his wife, Concepción, who were asleep in their home in Panaj canton. Gaspar was a former seminarian from the parish, a prominent Tz'utujil catechist, and the director of its radio station, the Voice of Atitlán. The fact that his program, "Christ Calls You," aired three times a day, every day, was one more reason that he was a well-known Tz'utujil in the region.

Concepción remembered waking up first, then waking up Gaspar, who jumped to his feet at the sight of the men and began screaming for someone to help him. He was struck right away by the butt of a gun and pushed down to the floor, where the men viciously stomped on him. His screams for help quickly changed to a pleading: "Go ahead and kill me quickly!" Gaspar yelled.

Hoping to avoid the intruder's attention, Concepción pulled their one-year-old daughter, María Linda, to her chest, holding her close and trying to keep her quiet. Someone pointed a flashlight at her face and fired a gun in her direction, but missed. Concepción watched in horror as the men dragged Gaspar out of the hut, with a noose around his neck. The attackers left the door open, Gaspar's bloodstains on the wall, and Concepción crying in the darkness. His body was never found.

Years later, when Concepción told the story about that night, she emphasized that Gaspar was never connected to the guerrillas. "Padre Francisco was a very good person," she said, and Gaspar and Padre Francisco worked closely together. "The people in the town suffered a lot when the soldiers were here," she added quietly. Gaspar was the first Atiteco taken from their village, but many more followed.

"Our situation here is steadily getting worse here in our town," Father Stanley wrote on November 4, 1980, to Archbishop Salatka, in a letter describing their state of affairs:

> Two men were taken from their homes and vanished. It is rumored that one has returned, but it is not certain. The next night, the director of the radio was taken and it is reported that he left the house unconscious.
>
> Sunday afternoon another was taken for a possible traffic violation and hasn't been seen again. Monday night a member of one of the co-ops was taken. By this time the people are literally scared to death. As a result, hundreds of people come to the Church to sleep for the night. Almost every night there are several catechists that come to spend the night with us to take turns standing watch. Last night the radio building was broken into, all the files rifled, and they lost four tape recorders and three typewriters. Luckily the three that were there to guard the building escaped.... Anyone who has made any advancement at all is being pursued. As a result we have any number of catechists that have left the area....
>
> I am a little tense tonight about where to sleep and whether to have someone stay here with me. The associate will be back tomorrow after leaving Sunday to get some rest.... I have no intention of leaving here yet. Four priests recently left from the Chimaltenango area of our diocese. Three were foreigners. I have had no indication as yet that some group wants me out. Usually

there will be some kind of direct threat in a letter or by word of mouth from someone in the know. My associate feels the tenseness more than I do, and we will probably go ahead and try for his visa.

Father Stan ended with a plea for prayers: "We can use an occasional prayer for our safety if that is the will of the Lord. I still don't want to abandon my flock when the wolves are making random attacks."

Father Pedro Bocel, who was the only priest of Indian blood in the Diocese of Sololá at the time, believed that it was precisely Father Stanley's closeness to the native Tz'utujil — including his ability to speak the language fluently — which made him stand out. Even though Father Stanley was not "giving strong messages, but only the Word of God" to the people, the fact that he was preaching in Tz'utujil was a threat to the military, which was made up of non-Indians. "The enemy thought he was putting bad ideas into the people's heads because he knew the language." But Father Stanley was merely "trying to live with the people … go to their houses … visit … help … meet with the cofradía leaders. [Padre Francisco] worried a lot about the people."

Orejas, Not for Listening

Disappointingly, some Tz'utujil used this brittle situation to begin turning in the names of other villagers to the government, out of sheer jealousy. The Bible translators, for example, were known to have a steady source of income from the parish. And one of them in particular, Juan Mendoza, had been the primary tutor for Father Stanley in learning the Tz'utujil language and had become his close friend. When people began randomly selling out other people, Father Stanley went to visit Juan. His wife, Candelaria, remembered how Father Stanley came asking Juan to help him better understand the cycle of violence unfolding in the village.

"For everyone in our family, Padre Francisco was more like a father," explained Candelaria. After discussing the dynamics of the situation and assessing its magnitude, Father Stanley advised Juan Mendoza to leave for the United States. But Juan refused to go without his family, and the family couldn't go with him. So Father Stanley decided to find a "safe house" to rent in Guatemala City, a place where the translator could live in safety and continue his important work on the Tz'utujil New Testament.

Truth be told, Father Stanley scorned the government informers. Yet in a confined setting, faced with few opportunities, and charged with intensifying panic, it is too easy for some people to act out of hatred and fear, with no concern for truth or facts. "Many people know who [the informers] are and they are salaried by the government. Some say they get 200 [quetzales] for a name they turn in as being dangerous to the state and should be eliminated," Father Stanley said in a letter to his archbishop. "There are as many as three different groups here and there is some indication that they are having troubles between themselves. I don't want to give any names, but later on some of these more important ones will almost certainly be liquidated. They can now walk the streets, not work, have money to spend, but justice will reign."

The *orejas*, or listening ears, were everywhere, remembered frequent volunteer Bertha Sánchez. "[Father Stanley] would receive word from time to time that people were watching him. Some of the *orejas* actually came into the rectory and asked him to do this or that. There was an aura of fear and intimidation. Part of it was jealousy," she said. "In that kind of atmosphere you learn not to say too much. It's sad when you are suspicious of even your neighbors."

In a letter to a priest friend some two weeks later, Father Stanley confessed his tired and weary state:

> The night after the radio station was broken into, I was by myself here in the house and I really let it get to me. I was so certain that they would do the same thing here, that I left all the doors unlocked so they wouldn't break them down, put the typewriters, money box etc. in the safe, and slept with my shoes on, staying in the living room and planned to lock myself in the bathroom when they arrived. Of course, nothing happened and I didn't get much sleep.

On Friday, November 7, the army officer in charge of the troops at Santiago Atitlán called the village's church leaders, pastors, and *cofradía* members to the mayor's office for a meeting. Once the group assembled, the officer walked into the room, pointed directly to Father Stanley, and asked him to translate what he was going to say in Spanish for the Tz'utujil. "He acted like he knew who I was, how long I had been there," Father

Stanley wrote two weeks later. The pastor refused and asked his associate Father Pedro Bocel to do it instead.

The officer began his discourse by stating that the army had come to Santiago Atitlán to protect the people from the guerrillas at large. They were there to help, he stressed, accentuating over and over the army troops' benevolent intentions. When he was done speaking, he opened the discussion for questions. Father Stanley seized the moment, immediately raising his hand. "My hand shot up like a jack-in-a-box … and among other things I told him that it would be hard for them to get the confidence of the people because all of this [kidnappings] started 2 days after they arrived and when certain ones were taken out of their houses, the whole area was surrounded by them," Father Stanley wrote to his Oklahoma friend Father Leven in a November letter. Apparently shocked by either Father Stanley's blunt statements or the fact that he was challenging his statements, the official confronted him by asking if he would rather be dealing with formal charges. Father Stanley replied that he was merely repeating what he had heard on the street. Throughout the exchange, the army officer managed to keep his composure, and he and Father Stanley even shook hands at the end of the meeting. On the other hand, the few evangelical Protestant ministers who were there lavished praise on the officer and his men for coming to their assistance and presented the commander with the gift of a Bible.

After the session broke up, the *cofradía* leaders approached Father Stanley and thanked him for speaking up. But his associate pastor was very nervous. "Padre Francisco told them the danger came when the army arrived," Father Pedro repeated, "and the colonel got mad." And when Father Pedro told his pastor that the colonel didn't like the comments he had made, Father Stanley replied, "It's the truth."

When Father Gregory Schaffer, the pastor of San Lucas, heard about the incident, he wasn't surprised. "He wasn't afraid of a thing … that Oklahoma farm boy in him was strong," Father Schaffer said, noting that he wasn't careless. Father Stanley, for example, reminded the radio station people when it was time to "calm down," he explained. "Stan was prudent."

An Unwanted Top 10 List

All over the Diocese of Sololá and the Lake Atitlán region, intimidation and fear were gradually transforming into terror and suffering. People were being taken from their families and never seen again, *desaparecidos* into certain death. And death lists became something common to talk about, as normal as exchanging sports standings of favored teams. For Catholic catechists, priests, and volunteers who lived there and worked hands-on with the Mayan poor, the question wasn't if but when they would be listed.

Father Stanley's friend and support-group member Father Ron Burke described the fateful day when he was traveling from Guatemala City to his parish at Parramos, and two very terrified parishioners stopped him. They told him that lay worker Pio Coban had been murdered, and that in Pio's hand he held a death list with the names of 81 people. Father Burke's name was number one. The San Francisco priest immediately

turned around and headed for the American Embassy in Guatemala City. At the embassy, when a U.S. Marine refused him
entrance, Father Burke unambiguously declared, "You might
find a body out here if you don't let me in." Not long after,
an armed escort took Father Burke to the Guatemala City
airport, and he departed the country where he had been a missionary for years.

Back in Oklahoma City, reports about the nightmare taking place in the Lake Atitlán highlands began arriving as early
as mid-November through various sources. Unfortunately, the
accounts carried both fact and fiction. One of the more distressing and inaccurate reports circulating Oklahoma was that Father
Stanley had been "taken." Even the very prestigious Amnesty
International had responded with an urgent public appeal on
Father Stanley's behalf.

So on Saturday, November 15, 1980, Bishop Melotto summoned Father Stanley to his residence, by request from the bishops of Oklahoma. Father Stanley crossed Lake Atitlán by launch
to Panajachel, where he telephoned Archbishop Salatka directly,
detailing to him the situation at Santiago Atitlán and assuring
him that they were all right. But Father Stanley still had no idea
that there continued to be a growing public uproar over his
safety, with rumors of his disappearance. And he did not specifically request that the archbishop contact his family. The following week, at the request of the American Embassy, Father
Stanley traveled to Guatemala City and answered questions from
officials there regarding the conditions in his village.

He also visited the Maryknoll House, where he learned of
an urgent request to telephone his parents in Okarche, Oklahoma. In a letter a week later to his sister, Father Stanley reported

what happened when he called home: "Mother started to cry when she recognized my voice and then I realized what you all had been thru." In another letter, about the same time, he complained about the lack of accurate information: "I wish people would get their facts straight before they start talking and cause a lot of grief and tears that aren't necessary."

The New Normal

"Life around here just hasn't been normal of late," wrote Father Stanley in a letter to his dear friend Frankie Williams. "I guess we will have to get used to it though. The government is desperate in maintaining control of the country, and they have more and more people working for them. But as it so often happens, the more the repression, the more the people rebel." Yet he remained optimistic, writing, "Fr. Pedro and I have been afraid like anyone else, but we are fine," and then added, "Most of our classes and other meetings are cancelled, and almost nobody is on the streets at night." Father Stanley also reported that farmers were neglecting their fields, and that market activity was minimal. Even the necessary tasks of hauling water and gathering firewood were kept to a minimum.

"Sometimes we even have to change the places where we sleep just in case they look for us," he continued. "But we have no direct information that we are being sought. The radio is no longer on the air, and most of the equipment is being stored.... All the workers there, some of the catechists and many of the leaders in town are in hiding in other parts of the country.... I guess we will get used to it little by little."

It is very difficult to assess how far circumstances — no matter how grave — shape and modify ordinary life, especially when those changes are gradual. After the first four kidnappings of October in Santiago Atitlán, there ensued a lull in overt terrorist activity. Yet nothing was normal about the mission's new normal. Conditions continued to bother the citizens of Santiago Atitlán, oppressing the people and withering their spirit without using blatant force. Then here and there, stories began to spread from one person to the next about another *desaparecido*, a villager who never made it home. Next, a body of a disappeared villager was found and quietly buried. Through his parish network, Father Stanley gathered information about the people he loved so much — information on possible whereabouts of parishioners on the run; the needs of women and children who were left behind; and locations of bodies of the *desaparecidos*, found murdered.

By December 2, Father Stanley reported there had been 10 Tz'utujil men "taken" from various cantons in the village. He began the somber work of searching for bodies, following any plausible rumors, such as "possibly three are buried in Chimal[tenango]." And he began the equally hazardous work of offering financial support and solace to the families of the missing or deceased men. When Juan Pachai Rujuch fled Santiago Atitlán, for example, he left out of loyalty to a family member, not an uncommon motivation for the Tz'utujil. When he arrived in Antigua, "those who killed" were waiting, according to Juan's wife, Juanita. Juan and three more Tz'utujil, all related, were taken — most probably tortured for information, and then presumably murdered. "We never found exactly where they were buried," Juanita recalled a decade later. "Padre Francisco looked for them." The sudden loss of her husband left Juanita with three small children and no means of support. The mother and one of the children had active cases of tuberculosis. And Father Stanley was soon at her door with consolation and practical help.

In addition to serving his people through the formal sacraments, the generous, loving pastor whom the Tz'utujil knew as "Apla's" himself became the presence and the oil that nourished and healed them. He fed the hungry. He sheltered the needy. He called on the Tz'utujil in hiding. He visited the persecuted in prison. He clothed and took care of the widows and fatherless children. And Apla's was hope for his people.

One of the times that Father Stanley drove Juan Mendoza's family to Guatemala City to visit the Tz'utujil translator at the safe house, someone took advantage of their absence to send the family — and Padre Francisco — a message. "They burned Candelaria's kitchen after she and two kids went to see him last week," he wrote in a letter, careful to scratch the real names of the people, aware that their mail was being monitored. "I had taken them and I was being followed yesterday on my way to Sololá. A National Police officer was with me and nothing happened." At some level, Father Stanley had to be conscious of the fact that this kind of activity was bringing attention to him and pushing the limits of his safety.

One essential thing, however, remained unchangeable — and that made all the difference for the loving pastor. "[O]ur presence here means a lot for the people," Father Stanley wrote to Frankie Williams. He continued:

When I hear the people during Mass here on Sunday or Thursday, the cacophony of prayers going up to the

Lord, His presence must be there. I am delighted to be a part.... At first signs of danger, the shepherd can't run and leave the sheep fend for themselves. I heard about a couple of groups of nuns in Nicaragua that left during the fighting and later wanted to go back. The people asked them where were you when we needed you? They couldn't stay and were forced to leave. I don't want that to happen to me. I have too much of my life invested here to run.

Eager for visitors from the north, Father Stanley wrote a letter to his sister, first, apologizing for the anxiety the family had suffered in fear for him, and second, offering assurances about his safety — and an invitation for her to come visit at Christmas time. "Thanks for your recent letter. It came at a time that I needed something from up there," he confessed to his beloved sister. "I also got one from the folks just before that and it had been two months since I had heard."

Father Stanley did not hide his hope that, in spite of the family's concerns, Sister Marita would come for an in-person visit. Even his statement admitting that mission "meetings and classes have been pretty much stopped now," was followed by, "[so] we will have more time to sit around and visit or travel." He concluded the letter by saying, "I am counting on your coming down.... You make your own decision to come or not, and if you don't I will understand. But we would like to have you visit."

In reality, Sister Marita noted, "I couldn't put my parents under that kind of stress," looking back on the situation in December 1980. "To have both of us there would not have been sensible. [Our parents] needed somebody here to support them. I knew what they were going through." During the scare caused by the unfounded gossip that Father Stanley had disappeared, "I had come down [from Wichita, Kansas], made a special trip to come see them [in Okarche]. It was really tough for them."

A Martyr of Charity

The Gospel of Luke tells the story of how Jesus, who was approaching the gate of Jerusalem, stopped when he saw a procession of people carrying a man who had died, the only son of his mother, who was a widow. When the Lord saw the widow, his heart was moved with pity for her and he said to her, "Do not weep" (Lk 7:13). Jesus then stepped forward, touched the coffin, and commanded the dead man to wake up.

Like Jesus, Father Stanley was moved with great pity for the widows, the mothers, and the children of the men who were taken, the *desaparecidos*, and the dead in Santiago. Yet in a setting where the people who were killed were considered subversives, the priest who helped the families of the dead was also labeled a subversive. Benedictine Father Patrick Greene described the situation this way:

> He tended to provoke the right by giving hospitality to those they thought were guerrillas and by helping the widows of guerrillas ... the army had the idea there [was] a military organization in the church.... [Stan] tried to do it openly. As a result, from the army's viewpoint, it

looked like he was favoring the left. That's why Bishop Melotto could say he was a martyr of charity.... There's a very, very fine line between Christian charity and moving people to be active against the government. It's almost impossible to make the distinction.

Father Stanley's former boss at the mission Jude Pansini emphasized years later that, without a doubt, Father Stanley never had links with the guerrillas and that there was "no way" he was a collaborator with them. Pansini, who came back to the Santiago mission regularly until he and his family had to leave the country, recalled Father Stanley's anger when a box of nails for puncturing tires was delivered to the rectory. He resented others trying to tar him with the guerrilla brush, said Pansini.

Father Adán García remembered Father Stanley's "big interest for the orphans and the widows. He was very preoccupied that the widows should have a written title [to the land]. He, with his own money, bought land and gave it to the widows," Father Adán recalled. Father Stanley was very concerned about the seven death threats that Father Adán received and wanted a bodyguard for the young priest. According to Father Adán, only he and Father Stanley knew about the "safe house" in Guatemala City, where Father Stanley took catechists who were in danger. Father Stanley was also very nervous about losing the New Testament books translated in Tz'utujil, Father Adán said, so "he decided to build a strong box of brick where the books and [our] wills would be kept." Receiving incessant threats, Father Adán finally left Santiago Atitlán in November 1980.

When the catechists began to disappear, Hermana María del Pilar remembered, "Padre Francisco was plenty worried. The situation kept getting worse and worse. People would come and spend one or two nights in the church.... He was always going out to help people who were sick, to help the widows, the poor," said Hermana María del Pilar, a Cakchiquel Indian from Patzun and a member of the Carmelite Missionaries who worked at the parish during that difficult period. She said, "They seemed to be persecuting Padre Pedro [Bocel], pursuing him."

Sololá's Bishop Angélico Melotto described Father Stanley as "simple," or perhaps innocent. Father Stanley's response to what was taking place all around him was to emphasize that "you must oppose this violence." Yet, to do that, the bishop noted, was to call attention that may have made the persecution of the Tz'utujil worse.

In his Christmas letter of 1980 to the Dioceses of Tulsa and Oklahoma City, published in both diocesan newspapers, Father Stanley tried to describe the Guatemala situation, taking care to clarify incorrect reports the Oklahomans might have heard about their Santiago Atitlán mission:

> I am sure that many of you have heard rumors and saw articles about our area during the past month or two. Some is true, sad to say, some exaggerated, some false, and some that hasn't been told. The purported reason for the presence of the army in our immediate area is to drive out and protect us from communist guerrillas. But there aren't any around here. A group did come into town in early June for about 2 hours and made some promises to those who were around. There seemed to be

interest on the part of some in their presence here. So far we have ten men that have disappeared … there is no set pattern for those being taken. In our town are a number of informers who are paid by the authorities to be spies, etc. [T]hey are paid for names turned in if these are later captured. The denunciations are sometimes because of envy, vengeance or just downright greed. A good friend of mine just happened to be in the wrong place when several others were picked up. He left a wife and three children … another man left seven children…. A nice compliment was given to me recently when a supposed leader in the Church and town was complaining that "Father is defending the people." He wants me deported for my sin.

This is one of the reasons I have for staying in the face of physical harm. The shepherd cannot run at the first sign of danger. Pray for us that we may be a sign of the love of Christ for our people, that our presence among them will fortify them to endure these sufferings in preparation for the coming of the Kingdom. Thanks to all of you for your support and prayers for us in the past weeks and months.

Although the group of Christmas visitors for 1980 was originally scheduled to include nurse Marcella Faudree and a companion, Sister Marita, and Frankie Williams, only Frankie made the pilgrimage to the mission in Santiago that year. The presence and love of the effervescent Frankie was no doubt much needed healing balm for Father Stanley's tired spirit.

Diego Quic

A mission success story, Diego Quic had become an educated, self-confident Tz'utujil — and a trained catechist active in many pastoral programs at the parish church. He and his wife, Juana, had two sons, ages one and three, and lived in a typical Tz'utujil hut in Xechivoy canton. By January 1981, 30-year-old Diego had also become the most sought-after catechist by the military, leading him to request asylum at the parish rectory. Father Stanley gave Diego a key to the house, and every afternoon the young catechist left to visit his family. Bewildered by his inclusion on the death list, Diego said to Father Stanley, "I have never stolen, have never hurt anyone, have never eaten someone else's food, why then do they want to hurt me and to kill me?"

One Saturday evening on his way back to the rectory after visiting his family, Diego was cut off by a group of four kidnappers. He was able to get within 15 feet of the rectory door while fighting three of the men, holding on to the porch banister while loudly yelling for help: "*¡Ayúdame!*" (Help me!). Inside the rectory, Father Pedro Bocel heard the commotion and looked outside to see what was going on. He thought about stepping in and trying to help, but he admitted later that he was scared by the assailants' height. Instead, Father Pedro ran inside and called out for Father Stanley, who was in the living room listening to music. "[B]y the time I realized what was happening, grabbed a jacket and got outside, they had taken him down the front steps of the Church and were putting him in a waiting car," Father Stanley wrote to Father John Steichen, the official contact of the Archdiocese of Oklahoma City with MICATOKLA.

In the process of dragging Diego away, the kidnappers and Diego had broken the banister where the rectory porch joins the Church. Father Stanley stopped where the rail was broken. "I just stood there wanting to jump down to help, but knowing that I would be killed or be taken along also. The car sped off with him yelling for help but no one able to do so. Then I realized that Fr. Pedro, Frankie Williams from Wichita and I had just witnessed a kidnapping of someone that we had gotten to know and love and were unable to do anything about it," Father Stanley wrote with a dazed tone. "They had his mouth covered, but I can still hear his muffled screams for help. As I got back in the rectory I got a cramp in my back from the anger I felt that this friend was being taken off to be tortured for a day or two and then brutally murdered for wanting a better life and more justice for his pueblo."

Soon after the car sped away from the plaza, the stunned group from the mission walked the area and found Diego's hat in front of the church and his right shoe at the bottom of the steps. Someone found a hand grenade on the church porch, apparently dropped by one of the kidnappers. Right away, Father Stanley walked to the village's telephone office and called the police in nearby San Lucas, asking them to keep an eye out for a car coming their way. He specifically stressed this was a kidnapping and that the kidnappers were armed. The San Lucas police replied they would see about it, "but they probably hid instead," Father Stanley wrote in his January 5 letter.

When Father Stanley returned from the telephone office, he suggested to the dazed group that they stand in a circle, hold hands, and pray — for Diego, for his family, and for peace for the village. Later, the group at the rectory drifted into the living room, where they sat mostly in silence, with only occasional comments. Father Stanley turned and said to Frankie, "I am so glad you are here and experienced this with us. You can go back home and tell people what happened."

Counting Diego Quic, "that makes 11 members of this community that have been kidnapped and all are presumed dead," Father Stanley wrote in the letter to his friend, as if counting bodies, morgues, and places of burial were a normal topic for anyone. "Only one body has been positively identified and buried here; there are possibly three buried in a common [grave] in Chimaltenango. They were picked up in Antigua and the following week I went to all the hospitals and morgues in the area and got a list of their characteristics and clothing.... For these 11 that are gone, there are eight widows and 32 children among the group. These people are going to need emergency help."

Perhaps writing in a stream of consciousness, trying to make sense of the senselessness, Father Stanley continued the letter by listing the parishioners affected by the violence who needed help: the widows, the children, the people who left for fear of their lives and couldn't find work in exile, parishioners who were salaried by the radio, artisan co-ops, health promoters. Still, "other towns in the diocese are being hit harder than us at the present," Father Stanley acknowledged. "In the past couple months three priests of the diocese have had to leave because of direct threats, and two others got scared and left. All but one were foreigners."

Days later, a close friend of Diego Quic came to the rectory to see Father Stanley, distraught, still in grief over the loss of his friend. Frankie remembered how "impressed" she was by Father Stanley's patience. "Stan stood there for an hour with his arms around this man, listening," she remarked, amazed by her friend's ability to "console a person with such tenderness and patience."

On January 7, 1981, Father Stanley drove Frankie to Guatemala City's La Aurora International Airport. At the passport clearing area, beyond which non-passengers were not allowed to go, Father Stanley looked at Frankie and said, "Do you think Diego knew I couldn't help him?"

"He had tears in his eyes," she remembered. "I never saw him in a full-fledged cry."

A Bloodbath in Atitlán

As painful and shocking as Diego's abduction was, a tragedy of even bigger proportions was taking place at Santiago Atitlán while Father Stanley was in Guatemala City dropping off Frankie at the airport. Although the exact details of how that tragic January 7th unfolded are difficult to piece together, it apparently began when an army truck on the road between Santiago Atitlán and Santa Clara la Laguna hit a tree mine, presumably placed as part of a planned ORPA ambush. Immediately, the soldiers traveling in the army convoy jumped out of their vehicles and began shooting toward the coffee fields, killing in retaliation "everybody they could get ahold of," described Dr. John Emrich.

Dr. Emrich, the Project Concern volunteer, had already sent his children out of Guatemala, but he had remained working at the hospital with his wife, Susan. Evidently, with a military helicopter hovering over the bay, the army company basically went on the offensive and began shooting everyone in sight. One group of soldiers headed into the coffee fields, and another went to nearby San Antonio Chacayá.

"Suddenly we heard our dogs barking wildly and the military appeared. They came sweating and panting, as if someone were pursuing them," recalled one of the San Antonio Chacayá witnesses.[20] "There were many of them, perhaps 100 and their faces were angry, in addition to being afraid of someone, because they kept looking in all directions." They detained every person they came across; some were tortured, others executed. "They kicked them, hit them, hit their heads and mouths with gun butts, they stood on top of them. Some of them choked on the dust that was rising from the ground."[21]

When it was over, the dead included: the Ladino manager of Finca Chacayá and two others who were with him in his truck; two teachers on a motorcycle, both executed after army personnel tortured them; a Tz'utujil fisherman who laid down in his small boat when the shooting began; and a group of perhaps 11 Tz'utujil campesinos who were discovered hiding from the gunfire in a stone hut. Some of the campesinos in the hut were taken away alive by the military, tortured for information, and then killed. Seven bodies of the tortured were discovered later on the east end of Lake Atitlán.

According to a United Nations report, 18 defenseless civilians were arbitrarily executed, and at least four were tortured by members of the military that day, in what came to be known as *la masacre del pato* ("The Duck Massacre"), because the victims were caught as they carried out their everyday tasks such as hunting ducks on the shores of the lake.

"At nightfall Santiago Atitlán was filled with sorrow, with weeping, with sadness and also with fury. No one believed what had occurred."[22]

One after another, the bloody bodies were carried into town and set down on the municipal plaza at Santiago Atitlán. For the families of the dead, who were laid out like decorations across the stoned plaza, the anguish was doubly exacerbated by the accusation that came with claiming their loved one's body. To put it another way, for a woman to assert a relationship to one of the men already judged guilty by being savagely murdered, it was equivalent to branding herself a subversive.

As Padre Francisco walked across the church plaza and down the steps to the municipal plaza, the packed crowd separated to allow him access to the bodies. With armed soldiers and their officers monitoring him, the Tz'utujil waited silently for any clue from their pastor. Finally, one brave Tz'utujil woman stepped forward and pointed to a corpse. "This is my husband," she said. Without any need for explanation, the woman became aware that Padre Francisco had walked over to stand beside her. And he waited for the next Tz'utujil to take the lead. Every time someone stepped up to claim a body, their faithful pastor walked over and stood with them.

For most of the women in the crowd, however, the fear for their lives and for their families was paralyzing, and many could not bring themselves to identify the corpses of their spouses. At the end of the evening, Father Stanley ordered seven of the bodies to be carried into the church, and he arranged for coffins to be made for each of them. One of the Santiago Carmelite sisters who was present described what she observed about Father Stanley during those days: "[Padre Francisco] cried a lot. It was the first time I had seen him cry. He felt very powerless. He couldn't do anything." Nothing, except stand in tender communion with his suffering flock.

"What Can I Do?"

Later that same week, Father Stanley drove to Panajachel for one of the diocesan meetings of the priests, pastoral workers, and sisters working throughout the Diocese of Sololá. At one point during the gathering, a determined Father Stanley stood up to address the group — begging them to make a clear and public condemnation of the oppression and violence being carried out against their communities. He proposed an official statement from the bishop, to be backed up by the signatures of every one present there.

Everyone there knew what the Oklahoma missionary had been through during those previous two weeks: the abduction of his friend and catechist Diego Quic, and the massacre of his Tz'utujil parishioners that had taken place just two days earlier. And many of these diocesan workers and foreign missionaries had suffered similar killings in their own parishes.

American Sister Tonia Marie Orlando recalled the awkward silent response at the meeting. "He stood up and said, 'What am I to do? What can I do?' He felt powerless, desperate, and sad. He loved his people very, very much."

Bishop Angélico Melotto, who felt coerced into making an immediate decision by Father Stanley's blunt request, remembered that event vividly. "I remember one occasion, when the violence started, a meeting of the priests and sisters. [Father

Stanley] wanted to make a public condemnation," the bishop said, pausing, recalling that delicate moment a decade later. "If you were too clear, the persecution [against the people] might be worse."

"I heard him stand up and ask for some kind of response from the Church in Sololá in the midst of the violence," recalled Sister Linda Wanner, a newbie who had only been at San Lucas Tolimán for four months. "Nobody responded to what he was asking. [Finally] a Maryknoll Sister stood up and said, 'We can raise some money.' Everybody seemed so spooked and paralyzed," she described. "He just impressed me as a man so concerned about the people, all of them … the whole image of the shepherd becomes so real … you could see the pain in his eyes."

A few days later, on an overnight trip to Guatemala City for supplies, Father Stanley was informed by a friend that he and Father Pedro Bocel were in grave danger — and that it was imperative that they leave the country immediately. Thanks to the efforts and quick initiative of fellow-missionary Father Gregory Schaffer, Father Pedro was brought to Guatemala City to meet up with Father Stanley. And the two men immediately began the taxing process of obtaining a U.S. residency visa for Father Pedro.

Like fugitives hiding from bounty hunters, the two mission priests went underground for the next 16 days. Aided by some of their Tz'utujil parishioners who were already in hiding in the capital city, the two priests moved from place to place, while continuing to push the embassy for a resident visa for Father Pedro from every angle possible. Finally, on January 28, 1981, an official from the American Embassy escorted the men to the airport, where they boarded a plane headed for Houston. In a newspaper interview two months later, Father Stanley admitted to a reporter: "Before I left I got permission to leave and to return" from the Guatemalan government.

When the two priests landed in Oklahoma City's Will Rogers Airport that January day, Father Stanley walked off the plane wearing a short-sleeved shirt and carrying a briefcase as his only baggage. As soon as she reached him, Gertrude Rother embraced her oldest son and kissed him, as Franz tried to hide the anxiety he'd been carrying for days with a slight smile.

Stanley Rother's Garden of Gethsemane

If his time working at Lake Texoma building cabins for the Oklahoma Church was his time of preparation in the desert, the months Father Stanley spent back in Oklahoma in early 1981 were, in a very real way, his Garden of Gethsemane.

From the onset, Father Stanley thought it important to make it clear to family and friends that their presence in the States was temporary. He and Father Pedro planned to return to Guatemala as soon as it was safe to do so. While he was away from Guatemala, Father Stanley had arranged for his friend, veteran Maryknoll missionary Father Ed McClear, to look after Santiago Atitlán on the weekends. But this arrangement was clearly provisional.

On the outside, Father Stanley took pause to recover physically and mentally from the strain and trauma of the past year at the mission. Inside, the pastor whose heart had been torn open with pain and empathy for his suffering Tz'utujil was still bleeding. He made time to see childhood friends and celebrate Mass with family friends. He worked at the farm alongside his youngest brother, Tom. He read as much as he could get his hands on, anything that would help him connect with Guatemala and gain information on the raging political situation there. And he prayed, surrendering himself and his life to the God of All, perhaps like never before.

During this period of exile from his beloved Tz'utujil, Father Stanley traveled Oklahoma and Kansas, taking time to visit friends and family. He visited David and Tina Iven twice, not only because David had been a member of the mission team but also because Tina was from Santiago Atitlán and she was mourning the loss of her brother, who had been shot to death in the January massacre outside the village. Her cousin's husband had also been murdered that day on the same mountain road. Father Stanley also traveled to eastern Oklahoma to see Father Herman Foken, and to Oklahoma City to visit mission volunteers Joe and Mary Tinker.

In Wichita, Kansas, Father Stanley made long visits to his dear friend Frankie Williams and to the Adorers of the Blood of Christ community. When he stopped by the motherhouse of the Adorers of the Blood of Christ, Father Stanley was the center of attention in a crowd of sisters who knew him well — some had taught him in Okarche, others were longtime friends of the Rother family, and several had been volunteers at the Santiago Atitlán mission. When the conversation turned to Guatemala, Father Stanley described, with honesty and emotion, some of the horror stories and pain that he had witnessed. One of the sisters turned to him and said, "But, Stan, you might be in heaven by Easter!" In response, Father Stanley smiled and said, "Can you think of a better place to be?"

Back in Okarche, two of his close high school mates, Harold and Ralph Wittrock, drove out to the Rother farm to see Stanley. "We visited and reminisced together" until the early hours of the morning, noted Ralph. But no matter what turns the conversation took, their priest friend always went back to the same topic, the mission, and "how the people were so spiritual but so mistreated." After hearing a few stories on the violence and the suffering, said Ralph, "It shocked me that he was this dedicated, this happy. I thought, 'Stan, you are something special.' " Speaking frankly to his lifelong friend, Father Stanley said, "I need to be with my people." As Ralph finally concluded, "That was his home. That's where he belonged."

To Harold Wittrock, that night on the farm allowed the two friends to have "the best discussion we ever had." Although Stanley seemed "agitated by the political climate down there," said Harold, he was grieved by the "atrocities" and "the burden on his poor people. He was resolved." Ultimately, Stanley confided in his friend, "I know it's a dangerous place, but that's my life … if it's to be, it's to be."

During those months he spent in Oklahoma, Tom Rother remembered that his oldest brother "seemed real uneasy.… He was always looking for something to do to keep busy. We were cleaning out some ponds [at that time], to get the silt out, and he came out here and helped with the job." With the air of a proud sibling, Tom added, "I can see why he loved [being in the mission] … he saw a need and he filled it."

Father Stanley also went to see the two Oklahoma Catholic bishops whose dioceses sponsored the mission. "When I last saw him here, there was his great determination to go back there," remembered Oklahoma City's Archbishop Charles Salatka. "He didn't want to die. He knew the risk was great. I couldn't help but admire him."

Tulsa's bishop at that time, Eusebius Beltran, who is now archbishop emeritus of Oklahoma City, remembered being "very impressed with Stan, his zeal, and his sincerity," when he first met him. "He was happy doing mission work. He talked about the difficulties, but he was very enthusiastic." During his 1981 visits, however, "He was kind of distraught at the time," Bishop Beltran said, remembering his two visits with Father Stanley during those months. "He told me he was so unhappy. He felt he should be in Guatemala. He asked me what I thought. I told him, 'I think you belong back there.' " Bishop Beltran explained that he thought of Father Stanley as he does about his sister, a missionary in Liberia. "Missionaries should stay with their people. That was the last time I ever saw Stan."

At some point during those three months, Christian Brother Mark Gruenke, from St. Paul, Minnesota, whom Father Stanley had never met, wrote a letter to the Oklahoma missionary when he found out that Father Stanley was in the States. Brother Gruenke had spent the previous summer as a volunteer in the health clinic of the San Lucan Tolimán Mission. He invited Father Stanley to go on a national speaking tour, giving presentations on the heartbreaking reality of Guatemala. "At this point I have mixed emotions.... I had to leave Santiago Atitlán following the massacre of 16 people on January 7th," Father Stanley wrote in a letter to Brother Gruenke dated March 3, 1981. "After working there for 12 ½ years, I feel almost like a Guatemalan and I still want to return. That is the reason I have mixed emotions about getting involved in a solidarity committee.... I want to return soon, but then I might not be given the choice to escape again." In the end, Father Stanley wrote, "The big question is — should I take a chance and go back? Nobody has yet convinced me to stay here. So until I decide definitely not to go back, I cannot get publicly involved in solidarity." A week later, Father Pedro Bocel left Oklahoma. He returned to Guatemala, but not to Santiago Atitlán.

Father Stanley made a visit to Mount St. Mary's, his old seminary in Emmitsburg, Maryland, where he met up with his classmate, now Archbishop Harry Flynn. "[Stan] told me terrible things that were happening to the Indian people," including a group of Indians who had been shot to death outside the village, recalled Archbishop Flynn. During that visit, he said, Father Stanley spent his days in the chapel, at his beloved Marian grotto, and walking the Stations of the Cross. "He said to me, 'If I stay there and speak I will be deported or killed,' "Archbishop Flynn recalled. "At the end of the week he told me, 'I know what I have to do.' It was like the Lord in the Garden of Gethsemane."

Oklahoma priest Father Thomas Boyer remembers well the last time he saw Father Stanley. "There was a small group of priests who got together for dinner at the Pastoral Center, a very informal dinner, with Archbishop Salatka. There were a lot of questions, many of them political," Father Boyer says. "Stan had the answers. He didn't seem to be threatened or afraid. I got the sense that he thought they were not in any great danger at that time — or he played down the reality of the threat."

In a very real way, "it's hard to think about Stan without thinking of Guatemala," said Father Boyer. "To me, he is Guatemala. He became the best of what that culture has to offer."

His friend Father Don Moore recalled the conversation he had with Father Stanley about returning to Guatemala: "Stan said to me, 'Everybody's told me I shouldn't go back but you haven't told me.' I told him that I didn't want him to return, but that I would support what [he decided to do]." In response, Father Stanley said to his friend, "I promised the people I would be back for Holy Week and I'm going to be there." Ultimately, said Father Moore, "in my heart of hearts, I think I knew [if he returned] he was going to be killed."

Sister Marita remembers vividly those final weeks that the missionary spent in Oklahoma. She traveled to their family home in Okarche to spend some one-on-one time with Stanley. As was customary for the two siblings who "never had to say a whole lot to know how we felt," Sister Marita remembers that her brother "wouldn't talk much about it all." At one point, however, "I did say to him, 'You know what you're doing to Mom.' And he replied, 'She'll be okay. She'll be okay. But this is what I have to do.'"

Sister Marita had seen her brother in action at the mission. She witnessed with her own eyes a man who gave himself completely to the Tz'utujil and to the mission work, and she knew that's where he belonged. Yet knowing the danger that awaited her beloved brother there, "just once" she had to say the words, "So, don't go." Father Stanley must have smiled back at her with eyes that said everything without using words. Remembering his simple reply, "But I have to," Sister Marita says now, "And that was it. I knew enough about God's working to know that when it's there, you've got to do it."

Before he left, Father Stanley discussed with his father the worst possible scenario: "Several times Stan said he had his escape route figured," Franz Rother recalled. "He had put a thicker, more sturdy door on the front of the house. He planned to go out the bathroom window into the courtyard to escape." Having seen the gruesome remains of a number of the Tz'utujil who had been taken and tortured — castrated, skinned alive, eyes punched out, all in the quest for information, Father Stanley must have also discussed with his dad that his ultimate plan was to fight with all the strength God gave him: "They'll never get me out of the rectory!"

It's true that Father Stanley's conversations with friends and family during those months seemed to constantly revolve around the question of *whether* he should return to Guatemala or not. Looking back on those comments now, however, the discussions and statements seem to be made by a man saying good-bye — the things that someone would say reaching out in love to his friends and family. Maybe the people he held close would understand why he had to go, or maybe they never would.

But like Jesus in the Garden of Gethsemane, during those decisive months back in the United States, Father Stanley opened his heart to each person he visited, and he asked those who were dearest to him to just *be* with him there.

The Letters

On March 22, 1981, two weeks before leaving Oklahoma, Father Stanley celebrated Mass and gave a talk at St. John the Baptist Church in Edmond, a commuting city just north of Oklahoma City. Although he had turned down other invitations to speak in public, he agreed to this one because his good friend Father Marvin Leven was the pastor.

It's safe to assume that at the homily that Sunday Father Stanley presented Guatemala through the eyes of his own stories and experiences, relating details about his beloved parishioners, and about the violence and relentless suffering experienced by the poor Tz'utujil who were the mission at Santiago Atitlán. It was a topic he was passionate about, and he had plenty of powerful anecdotes to tell.

After Mass, one or two discontented listeners accosted Father Stanley. He recalled the incident later, "I got through and one man walked up and said, 'I don't agree with anything you say'... the fellow said, 'I'm sorry I am a Catholic. I'm going to inform the archbishop.'"

About the Edmond experience, Father Stanley confessed to his friend Father Don Moore, "a few of them really tore into me." Sometime later he showed Father Moore a copy of the letter that had been sent to the archbishop, explaining, "I cannot let my parents see this letter."

In addition to the letter to the archbishop, an unsigned letter was sent addressed to the "Embassy of Guatemala, Military Attaché," in Washington, D.C. The author of the letter detailed a long list of grievances and criticisms, noting, "Our local pastor, a frequent visitor to your nation, invited a Catholic mission priest from Guatemala, to use God's pulpit to expound a political dogma urging our local church members to pressure the present U.S. government administration into allowing our country to decline military support for your current administration in Guatemala, in order to provide the basis for a socialist revolution which would oust the current government of Guatemala...."

"In as much as the Catholic Church is using the altar of 'God' to influence the Catholic populace in the United States, I feel obliged to warn your Nation's government of the church involvement within the leftist organizations attempting to establish a socialist government in Guatemala.... In conclusion, I will no longer offer monetary support for any overseas Catholic endeavors, but will instead forward this currency to those political action groups that support non-socialist governments of the Americas."

To all who knew Father Stanley, nothing could be further from the truth. "Stan was about as apolitical as a man can be ... that letter left him absolutely vulnerable," Father Don Moore emphasized years later.

In reality, Father Stanley's words in Edmond were in fact well received by many of the more than 1,000 people who heard him, including Father Leven and Dr. and Mrs. James and Corinne Lauridson, who also wrote a letter to Archbishop Salatka, stating:

> On Sunday March 22 [1981] we were fortunate in attending a Mass offered by Father Stanley Rother at St. John the Baptist Church in Edmond. Father Rother delivered a homily that dramatically described the plight of our brothers in Latin America. His life is an example of the true social meaning of the Gospel and the deeper implications of the Way of the Cross.

Yet the damage had already been done. It was the opinion of Archbishop Salatka that the complaint to the Guatemalan Embassy "put Stan on the black list in that area."

Coming Home

When he arrived in Guatemala that April of 1981, Father Stanley touched base with people he knew at three places before heading to Santiago Atitlán. First, he sought out and found Ray Gonzales, a political officer at the U.S. Embassy in Guatemala City and a man well trusted by American missionaries in Guatemala as someone who was in the know, and who would be honest about the situation. Gonzales told Father Stanley not to go back to Santiago Atitlán because it was too dangerous.

He also stopped by to see his friends, the Benedictine monks in Sololá. The community had in the previous year provided refuge — simultaneously — for people being persecuted from the left *and* the right. There was a monk there who was Father Stanley's information source regarding safety in the region. But unknown to Father Stanley, the Benedictine's contact inside the government was already unreliable. From the Benedictine priest, Father Stanley got the go ahead to return to Santiago.

Finally, Father Stanley met in person with Sololá's Bishop Angélico Melotto, at his home in Panajachel, across the lake from Santiago. "I told him, 'Don't go back to Santiago Atitlán now,' " the bishop remembered years later. "It is too dangerous." According to Bishop Melotto, Father Stanley heard him and responded, "My life is for my people. I am not scared," and the bishop did not forbid the missionary's return.

On the Saturday before Palm Sunday, as he set off on a *lancha* from Panajachel to Santiago Atitlán, Divine Providence arranged for Father Stanley to share the boat ride with 17-year-old Cristóbal Coché, the Tz'utujil seminarian from Santiago

whom Father Stanley had encouraged toward the priesthood
years before. As they crossed the lake on the one-hour launch
ride, Father Stanley let Cristóbal know how happy he was to
see him, but he also stressed to the young seminarian that it was
too dangerous for him to be seen on church property except for
Mass and Holy Week services.

"Why did you come back?" Cristóbal asked his pastor.
Speaking in Tz'utujil, Father Stan replied, "The pueblo needs
me, and I want to be here." Fifteen years later Father Cristóbal
Coché considered these words. "In his manner and way of speaking, he didn't seem too frightened, but he knew he was being
controlled, being watched. He was filled with some anxiety."
The last thing that Cristóbal remembered Father Stanley saying
to him was, "I don't know what is going to happen. If things get
really bad again, I will return to the United States."

As soon as Father Stanley stepped off the boat and onto the
dock, he could hear the shouts of "Apla's! Apla's!" as his surprised
parishioners welcomed him back to the village. The first place
that the pastor entered in the church complex was the convent,
where the Carmelite sisters were shocked to see him but joyous
at his surprise return in time for Holy Week.

One of the sisters later remembered the day Padre Francisco
returned: "When he was in the United States, we were there in
that very conflictive time. The military burned the fincas. The
sisters said if he returns, they will kill him. He knew the sisters
did not want him to return. He didn't tell us he was coming. He
surprised us." Through the sisters, Father Stanley found out that
the army at the edge of Santiago had doubled in the size of its
troops, bringing the number to 600 soldiers.

For Holy Week that year, both pastor and congregation must have thrown themselves into the commemoration and celebration of Christ's death and resurrection with complete and unbridled fervor. Padre Francisco, their priest, had returned!

During Easter week, Father Stanley received news that his friend and support-group partner Father David Vavasseur had returned to his home diocese of Baton Rouge. Describing the situation years later, Father Vavasseur noted that it was his parishioners who convinced him on Holy Thursday to leave Santa Apolonia, a mission in the Sololá diocese:

> Everywhere I went that day, I heard [that I should leave] from people.... When the Indians start telling you that, you had better listen. We were all nervous on Saturday. Some young women catechists told me to get out of there. It seemed like every night somebody got killed. By Sunday, I was really nervous. By late Sunday afternoon, I decided I had to get out of there. We were all using the example of Stan who had left and come back.

Father Vavasseur found out later that on the day he left, a group of unfamiliar men had gone to the rectory looking for him.

As previously planned, Father Stanley returned to Oklahoma one last time on the second week of May to attend his cousin Don Wolf's ordination to the priesthood.

"I felt a definite connection to him and to the mission because of my burgeoning work with the Spanish-speaking, as well as because of the attention that was being focused on the violence and uncertainty there," remembered Father Wolf. "Being identified with the Santiago mission was important to me. This was also a time when I was following very closely what was going on in El Salvador with the death of Archbishop Romero and the American sisters. The eyes of the whole world were turned in that direction. Stan was a window through which I could see and understand; his presence was a moment I could pour my awareness into."

Father Stanley didn't act gloomy or preoccupied, and he didn't discuss any concerns for his safety, Father Wolf said. "In fact, he seemed completely at ease with himself and with the guys around him. And that was the Stan I always knew.... He wasn't striving to be something other than what he was. He seemed to carry an air of peace around himself. Others were peaceful with him; I certainly was. It was more than familiarity; it was a genuine knowledge of self and, I think, real holiness."

After he returned to Guatemala, Father Stanley promptly sat down and drafted a letter to his newly ordained cousin. "May your priesthood be for you a source of much joy and a cause of salvation for many," the letter began, paraphrasing Archbishop Salatka's comment near the end of the ordination Mass. The letter continued:

That is also my wish and prayer for you. I thank God for the opportunity to be present and participate in your ordination Mass and Mass of Thanksgiving.

You might be interested in visiting here sometime. It is more safe for a visitor than for some of us working here. I think you would enjoy getting to know this area and it wasn't all kidding what I told the Archbishop as we formed the procession for your ordination. I know you would enjoy working here. But maybe that can be later, after a few years of experience. My associate still can't be here with me now. It would be nice to have someone here to have daily Mass and be around for sick calls etc. Then I could be in and out on an unscheduled basis and feel safer.... Take care, pray for me.

While things at the mission seemed to be calm, the general situation in Guatemala was anything but peaceful. The disappearances of laypeople continued. The first Guatemalan priest, Father Carlos Galvez Galindo was shot to death as he approached his church in Tecpan for a baptism, only a few miles from Santa Apolonia. And an Italian Franciscan and his catechist had been gunned down in Izabal as they headed home from Mass at one of the fincas, bringing the number of priests murdered in the country to seven over a 13-month period. In a letter to friends wherein Father Stanley listed the deaths, he surmised: "Sound like persecution?" The total number of priests in Guatemala plummeted from 600 in 1979 (80 percent of whom were foreign missionaries) to approximately 300 in 1981.

Summertime in the Village

In the summer months of 1981, the mission would normally have been buzzing with activity in preparation for the annual parish and village Fiesta for the feast of St. James the Apostle at the end of July. But the number of catechists in the mission had been severely depleted by murders, abductions, or catechists going into hiding. And the remaining catechists were understandably paralyzed with fear. After preparing and receiving a group of 149 for Confirmation on Pentecost Sunday, Father Stanley called a general meeting of all remaining catechists. Finally, "I just had to order them to do [the preparations]," Father Stanley described in a letter to his friend Frankie Williams, "and it is really amazing how it has helped the Catechists themselves and the parish in general."

"The nuns are fine," the pastor reported to Frankie, showing his pride and delight at the presence of the nine Carmelite Missionaries of St. Teresa, most of them indigenous Cakchiqueles. He then added:

> Sister Ana María Gonzalez left on July 2nd for two weeks in Mexico. She had to give a retreat to one group and the up-date to others. She is good at that and is called upon at times. The other Sisters are busy about their work; two go to Junior High full time, other two are taking correspondence. They prepare the parents and sponsors each week for Baptism … they have done so much for the music also in the Church. It is such a pleasure to have them there to organize the singing, have different banners, etc. for times that we hadn't prepared as yet. Two always go with me to Cerro de Oro for the Saturday Evening Mass.

That year, a record high 101 couples had their marriages witnessed by Father Stanley at the St. James the Apostle Fiesta, and over 200 Tz'utujil received First Communion. "All this work," he wrote in a letter to friends and mission volunteers Mary and Joe Tinker, "has done a lot to get the parish in gear again and to dispel some of the fear of the past months." At the mission rectory, the younger brother of Father Pedro Bocel, Francisco, had moved in to do cleaning, yard work, and help with the evening meal. "At least I'm not alone," Stanley stated in a letter.

One of Father Stanley's best qualities, according to his sister, Sister Marita, is that "he was really good about gratitude" — an opinion reinforced by the sheer number of letters and notes written by Father Stanley to say thank you: for visits, donations, financial aid, a good talk, for letters, or a meal. "I want to thank all of you in the name of the families who will benefit from this help for your kindness and generosity," he wrote on July 13, 1981, to the "Over 55" Club at St. Charles Borromeo Church in Oklahoma City, after their donation to the mission's orphan fund. "Surely this is evidence that you are fulfilling the plea from Christ that says: 'When I was hungry, you gave me to eat; when I was thirsty, you gave me to drink....' This is one of my favorite scripture quotations and I often use it for funerals. Here with these orphans I feel you will find 'one of the least of these brothers of mine.' Matthew 25:31."

On July 14, Father Stanley traveled to Guatemala City by bus in order to recover the mission's white pickup truck, stranded there since the missionary's abrupt exodus in January. While in the capital city, Father Stanley made a point of dropping by the National Palace to complain to the office of the Guatemalan minister of the interior about the recurring break-ins at the Voice of Atitlán radio station building, causing its equipment to disappear.

By far the most pleasant part of that trip was picking up mission nurse Bertha Sánchez at the airport. Bertha was coming to celebrate the Fiesta with Father Stanley and to spend a couple of weeks at the mission. Looking back years later at what she experienced when she arrived that summer, Bertha noted: "Stan was trying to be apolitical.... There was an aura of fear and intimidation. He was aware there were some sympathetic leanings for what the guerrillas were fighting for."

Like a volcano about to erupt, everything was different, even though nothing had changed. To say that anxiety was building in the village understates the powerful grip that the military's presence had over the people of Santiago Atitlán.

It was the Carmelite sisters who best described the unspoken tension that had been building in the village, in the parish — and in the rectory, how the catechists and the sisters took turns accompanying Padre Francisco anywhere he went around the village; how the rectory often had soldiers with automatic weapons stationed around it, with their guns pointed toward the rectory; how the sisters slept with their passports under their beds, and how difficult it was to sleep restfully; how Father Stanley had become the first one to rise in the mornings, with his lights on by the time the sisters woke up at 5 a.m.; and how they had organized recreation and prayer time together, to help defuse the tension.

"He was more intense in his prayer time," described one of the sisters. "We organized prayer times, and he prayed with us," said another sister. "Afterwards we played games to relax ... to make the nights less long. In recreation time," she recalled smiling, "Padre Francisco would dance with the sisters — or with a broom." Another sister pointed out that whenever they noticed any type of movement in the military troops or squadrons, "they had the strategy to ring the church bell."

During that time, no matter how risky, Father Stanley never stopped the practice of celebrating Mass at the fincas. "The roads are very difficult, and they were very dangerous at that time," remembered one of the sisters, "but we would still go, even though it could be for [only] five people. He didn't care how many people would be there."

The Hour Has Come

At some point around the July 25 Fiesta, Father Stanley traveled to Cerro de Oro to celebrate what would be his final Mass there. Cerro de Oro had been his first pastoral assignment with the Tz'utujil, and it was the first place that the Oklahoman celebrated the unique and elaborate ceremonies revolving around Holy Week and Easter Sunday in Guatemala. Without a doubt, the Tz'utujil community of Cerro de Oro had a special place in his heart.

Manuel Ajcabul Lacan, the lay president of the parish of Cerro de Oro, reconstructed years later his memory of Padre Francisco's final homily that July of 1981:

> Brothers, we have to keep on and fight for our Catholic Church. Don't lose your faith when you hear about violence. Some of you will die or be assassinated as it is in Santiago Atitlán, where the catechists gave their lives to defend the truth. I am not sad or worried that many of

the catechists in Santiago Atitlán are fleeing and others kidnapped or assassinated. There are many families with orphans and widows.

You are my catechists. Always meet. Don't forget your meetings to prepare the Word of God which I and the other priests teach you each week. Brothers, keep on with our pastor, Jesus Christ, and don't digress from the way and your faith. Support my catechists. My sisters and catechists, we will see each other in heaven. We have to be faithful before God and to the community. Follow in the faith of the saints and the apostles.

On Friday, July 24, the day before the feast of St. James the Apostle, Father Stanley was warned, directly and with certainty, that the government had decided to kill him. He had been summoned to San Lucas by his old associate pastor Father Adán García, who informed Father Stanley that his assassination was imminent. If he wanted to live, he had to leave Santiago Atitlán immediately. Father Adán remembered years later how he pleaded with his former pastor, saying, "Please come with me now and I will take you to the border! If you need your passport, get it now, and I will take you to the border!"

Father Stanley looked at his friend with gratitude and responded, "I will not leave the parish. I have a commitment to the people and to the sisters, and I will not leave." Father Adán persisted, begging Father Stanley to let him help, but Father Stanley replied once again, "No.... Don't worry. I will fight. They won't take me alive."

As soon as the townspeople heard that the military planned to use the July 25 festival to forcibly "recruit" men into the army, Father Stanley opened the church to provide sanctuary — and approximately 600 young men took refuge overnight in the building. That night, the army did not enter the church, perhaps acknowledging it as a safe haven.

In preparation for the Fiesta that year, Father Stanley helped the sisters decorate. "It delighted him" seeing the church so beautiful, noted one of the sisters, adding that the church decorations were still up for Padre Francisco's funeral Mass. To prepare the large church for the special Mass in honor of St. James, all the benches were removed from the building and the floor was washed. Rows and rows of see-through white material hung draped across the nave of the church, from one wall to the other, in crisscross fashion. Arches were set up and covered with cedar and pine, with fruits and flowers attached to them. The whole floor of the church, including the sanctuary, was carpeted with fresh pine needles, a symbol of new life and rebirth.

"One day we were joking [during the preparations] and he looked at me and said, 'When they kill me, don't cry for me. Put up the paschal candle and put up the Easter banner,'" emphasized Sister Herlinda Yos, one of the Carmelites. "He started all that, the experience of the Resurrection. That's why the liturgies are very solid in Atitlán. Padre Francisco invoked a sense of celebration in the liturgy.... Padre Francisco did speak out about dying. He said, 'If they come I'm not going to hide.' But he wasn't going to be passive; he would fight."

On either the Sunday before the Fiesta, or the day immediately after it, Father Stanley took everyone by surprise with his

straightforward words during the liturgy, remembered Hella Jaenike de De Paz, a German-Guatemalan teacher who was present.
"He said 'good-bye' with great emotion at Sunday Mass.… He
was very sad. He did say, 'If they kill me, praise be to God!' " —
adding that Father Stanley said to her, privately, "I'm not afraid
of dying. I'm afraid of being tortured," and of what confidences
— or confessions — he would be capable of betraying if he was
subjected to extreme physical cruelty.

According to Hella, Father Stanley had made plans with her
to bless her new home, but he was never able to go. "No one
was moving," she explained. "He knew he couldn't get out. The
army had a launch on the lake and people at the boats."

For dinner that Sunday night, Bertha volunteered to cook
one of her special Chinese spreads, and Father Stanley invited
the nine Carmelite sisters to the feast. Years later, the sisters remembered the distinctive invitation for that last supper together,
which included wine as an extra treat. "We began to play games
at the table," Sister Rosa Valentina Xinico Sipac recalled. "He
loved to beat everybody. Padre Francisco was joyful and happy."
In addition to dinner, Bertha made a large cake for the occasion,
which added to the upbeat atmosphere. "Padre Francisco said,
'You've got to keep eating this cake, else I will be eating cake all
week.' We were talking and talking," added the sister.

The following day, Monday, July 27, Cristóbal Coché Ajtzip,
who had been employed by Father Stanley as a night watchman
of parish property for two years, came to the pastor and told him
that he would not be able to work that Monday night because
one of his sons was ill. Cristóbal also warned his pastor that he
had overheard a rumor that there would be an attempt to kill
him that night. "You have a problem," Cristóbal told him.

That afternoon, Father Stanley firmed up plans to go to the Sololá hospital the next day to donate blood for a well-known man from Santiago who was having surgery to remove bullets from his hip. Sister Ana María Chavajay and Francisco Bocel agreed to go with Father Stanley, to make sure that between them, at least one would be eligible to give blood. After the hospital, Father Stanley and Sister Ana María planned to stop in Panajachel where a diocesan meeting of priests and women religious would be taking place.

As he normally did, Father Stanley celebrated Mass at 5 p.m. in the church, his final one. After Mass, Sister Rosa Valentina and Sister Herlinda Yos went with him to the market. As the three of them shopped for food, they noticed a quick thinning of the crowds. "Everybody dropped out of the plaza, as if afraid," recalled one of the sisters. It didn't take long for them to realize what was going on. The army was once again moving through the city streets snatching young men for forced military service. By the time Father Stanley and the sisters made it back to the church, there was already an assembly of young men requesting sanctuary.

Dinner that Monday night was around 7 p.m., with Bertha Sánchez and Francisco Bocel. After the meal, Father Stanley and Bertha moved to the living room, also known as Father Stanley's "safe room." "We were chatting and reading," Bertha remembered, when Francisco Bocel came to report that three more young men were "clinging to the wall" between the church and the rectory, asking to hide in the rectory for the night. The pastor went outside to talk personally to the threesome and "reluctantly" gave them permission, Bertha said. "I heard them go upstairs with Francisco."

"It was about 10:20 p.m., by my watch, when I said good night to Stan," Bertha said. It was just business as usual, "commenting that it was best to have an early night, if they were leaving early to donate blood for surgery."

This Is My Blood ...

The opening paragraphs of this book told how at 1:30 a.m., on July 28, 1981, three masked men broke into the rectory, found Father Stanley, and murdered him.

Two bullets hit his head from point-blank range. One entered his lower jaw and remained lodged in the bone on the opposite side. The other bullet, which was apparently the immediate cause of his death, entered his left temple and passed through the head, leaving a large exit wound on the right side of his skull. That bullet finally lodged in the floor.

He punched his attackers very forcefully, so much so that the skin was torn from his knuckles. In turn, the assassins repeatedly smashed their fists into the pastor's midsection. He had bruises on his body and on his hands, probably defense wounds from protecting himself against his assassins' blows. His head hit the wall and a large splotch of blood permanently marked the spot. His body was also mutilated prior to death by a torturer wielding a knife, yet Father Stanley never screamed or cried out for help, no doubt to prevent any would-be rescuers among the Carmelite sisters from being at risk.

"The moment we saw [the body of Padre Francisco] we began to pray," said Carmelite Sister María del Pilar Canux. "He had a T-shirt and trousers on, and he was lying on the floor, his face toward the door. It was obvious that he was dead." He had no shoes or socks. The blue knit sports shirt that the pastor had worn that night lay on the floor.

His eyes were slightly opened, an arm raised as in defense. "I remember trying to feel for his pulse," Bertha Sánchez recalled. "And I remember thinking, 'I don't know which way they went out.' " Bertha found herself thinking through the logistics and details that had once been their escape plan, as a way to discern how the attackers made their exit. Certainly no one came out through the courtyard. The only ways into the rectory on the ground floor were the front door, the dining room door, and the kitchen door. "I had a horrible feeling of helplessness."

Everything was splattered with blood. There was a huge pool of blood in the corner, where his head laid. A minute and an eternity later, Bertha Sánchez pronounced the pastor of the Tz'utujil dead.

CHAPTER 7

The Flesh of Jesus

The Tree Cried Out and Bled,
But It Did Not Die

The wooden altarpiece in the colonial-era church of St. James the Apostle is so beautifully crafted and so powerful in symbolism that the Tz'utujil have a legend to describe the story of its creation. The Atiteco myth goes like this:

——

A group of twelve powerful nuwal ancestors, six brothers and six sisters, climbed up the mountains to the place where the ancient gods reside in caves, and searched for a tree to watch over the saints. This tree would have to be willing to perform this duty. One after another, the trees refused ... until the cedar tree was asked, and it said yes. A split-log drum was played by the sisters while the brothers burnt incense in front of the tree and asked its spirit to continue living after it was cut down and fashioned into an altarpiece.

The first stroke of the axe slashed the cedar's trunk — and the tree cried out and bled. But the cedar did not die. As its wood was cut and sculpted, sacred songs and prayers accompanied the tree, giving it strength and vigor for its future mission. Finally, the saints were carefully positioned in the perfected altarpiece. And the wood of the cedar tree embraced and welcomed the saints, much as the mountains above and around Santiago shelter and protect the Tz'utujils' nuwals and ancient gods.[23]

—

The first Oklahoma missionary team began arriving in 1964. There were 12 missionaries to Santiago Atitlán. Like the ancestors in the Mayan myth, they were a group of six men and six women. Over the years, one after another, every one of them left the mission and its church, except one. A man strong as the cedar trees of his native Oklahoma, who was willing to watch over the saints — even when it meant he, too, would be cut down and bleed to death.

Unlike the simultaneous melodiousness of joyful voices lifting prayers during Mass that was so dear to Father Stanley's heart, the groundswell of murmurs sweeping through the village after his murder was pained and broken. Over and over the voices repeated the same ugly reality: "They killed him. They killed Padre Francisco...."

By the time Father Gregory Schaffer arrived in Santiago the morning of Father Stanley's death, the San Lucas pastor found "hundreds and hundreds" of Tz'utujil already gathered around the church. "A lot of talk, loud, and there was anger."

In spite of the mess and confusion, Sister Linda Wanner remembered going to the rectory's kitchen to look for utensils and receptacles that would help them clean and collect the blood that covered the room. After a short discussion, the women settled on a peanut butter jar and another large golden jar. They filled one jar with only Father Stanley's blood, and the other jar with blood-soaked gauze.

The Carmelite sisters took Father Stanley's body to the hospital to clean and dress him. Father Schaffer went to find the vestments. In tender and gentle ritual, they dressed him in Mass vestments, laying the *cofradía* shawl on his shoulders, the one he had been so proud to receive. Sister Rosa Valentina Xinico Sipac remembered a "special moment" in the hospital. As people were trying to dress the body, rigor mortis began to set in. They needed to move his bent arm, which was "in a defensive position," said Sister Rosa Valentina. "One of the nurses said out loud, 'Padre, help us. Please, help us,' and his arm relaxed.... The doctor who was there seemed speechless," Sister Rosa Valentina described years later. "Without a doubt he is a saint. We always invoke his name" in prayer.

Inside the big church, Sister Ana María Gonzalez led the people in singing resurrection songs. It was that simple act, believed Father Schaffer, which kept violence from erupting. "I'm convinced that kept people from an insurrection. Talk was not the low buzz of a crowd, but loud — and an insurrection would have resulted in many deaths. That's the last thing that Stan would have wanted."

There was a moment, recalled Father Schaffer, after Father Stanley's body had been laid in the church, when the masses of people simply wanted to be near their pastor. Father Schaffer's attention was suddenly captured by "a little old Indian woman, kneeling on the end of the pew and crying her heart out ... she kept repeating, 'They killed our priest. He was my priest, our priest … he spoke our language,' " he recalled. "Stan was just simply good, through and through…. I thought I had a close relationship to the people, but none of us were in the same league or even the same ballpark as Stan."

One of the main concerns of the Atitecos involved Padre Francisco's body. Father Stanley's family wanted to bury him in the Rother family plot at Holy Trinity Cemetery in Okarche. The Tz'utujil assumed that he would stay with them. They "didn't want to let the body go," Father Schaffer explained. "They didn't want his spirit to leave." Finally, a compromise was reached. Stanley Rother's body would be buried in Oklahoma. But his heart and his blood remained in the Santiago church where he belonged — where generations of Tz'utujil would honor and remember him.

And so it is more than symbolism that connects the Mayan legend about the cedar tree with the altarpiece and with the pastor of the Tz'utujil. Knowing this was his home, catechists dug a hole into the church floor behind the altar platform, directly under the carved altar screen Father Stanley had insisted on completing, and buried their pastor's precious heart there.

"They Killed Stan"

Word of Father Stanley's death spread to nearby villages immediately, rapidly, like the grass fires of his native Oklahoma fed by the infamous high winds that come sweeping down the plain.

Sister Bernice Kita, a Maryknoll missionary nun stationed across the lake from Father Stanley, still remembers well the toxic mix of shock and emotion. "[Stan] loved being a priest and pastor in Santiago Atitlán. He stood up for the people, and that's what got him killed. He was totally dedicated to the people."

In a letter to a friend a week later, Sister Bernice described her experience during those first moments after Father Stanley's death:

> There comes a time when you run out of tears. You catch yourself staring blankly out the window, shaking your head, as if that futile gesture could negate the escalating horror. "They killed Stan." These words were spoken in a broken voice by his friends, passed along to other friends.... Stan, with the face of St. Francis and a love and a dedication like Christ's.

> Stan, who by working the land with a hoe, earned the respect of the Indian men who love the soil. Stan, who, when asked if he was involved politically, replied: "To shake the hand of an Indian is a political act." Stan, probably the most peaceable of us all, and among the most courageous.

Father Stanley's coffin was brought up the main aisle in a solemn procession on the shoulders of members of Acción Católica, who were dressed in their best traditional Tz'utujil clothing. The procession also included two large jars, one containing Father Stanley's blood and the other the pastor's bloody gauze, in addition to a metal box holding the martyr's heart — all of which were ceremonially placed on the altar. "It was a powerful, powerful experience," Sister Linda Wanner, S.S.N.D., described. "You could just feel the sense of rightness of keeping the heart."

The long double line of mourners, described Sister Bernice, extended from the coffin near the sanctuary, overflowing through every exit and down the long church steps that lead to the town plaza, still decorated from the Fiesta. Most of the 2,000-plus had already been there for hours praying, singing, and crying together. Someone had donated wood to build the custom-sized coffin. None of the coffins in town were long enough to fit Father Stanley's long, thin frame. Sister Bernice continued:

> Inching forward with the mourners, I watched the men and women kiss the coffin as they filed past. Stan was a good-looking man with sandy hair, a neatly trimmed beard, and clear eyes. When I came to the coffin, I looked long at that face, now made unfamiliar by the violence that killed him. In farewell, I touched the rough wood of the coffin, still sticky from fresh varnish.

> When Mass began, the church was so packed that we could hardly move. All the benches had been removed. Men stood and women sat on their heels, in their accustomed way ... and practically all wore the distinctive costume of the Tz'utujil.

> At the moment of the consecration, there was a growing wave of murmuring, and a swell of voices drowned out the celebrant. I looked around me and saw tears

in every eye. On everyone's lips were the words: "Padre Francisco."[24]

There were two Masses celebrated in Santiago Atitlán before the body was taken to Guatemala City to be transported to Oklahoma: one in the evening and one the following morning.

The singing and praying that continued in the church throughout the night served to slowly soothe the clutching anger that witnesses note had been so palpable those first hours. After Mass the next morning, the body was moved in a procession from the church to an ambulance. When they drove away with the body of Padre Francisco, emphasized Sister Rosa Valentina, "we felt like the Bible says, like sheep without a shepherd," she added, crying. "There was a feeling of aloneness."

Father Schaffer will never forget the crowds and how difficult it was for him to drive out of town that day with Father Stanley's body. Over and over he would inch up in the vehicle and urge the people for space, "Please, let us go!" He drove at a snail's pace through the streets, clogged by the masses of people, until finally, he reached the road to San Lucas and Guatemala City. There, another Mass was celebrated at the cathedral before the body was flown to the United States.

Witness to the Living Christ
Present in His People

Five weeks after Father Stanley's murder, Bishop Melotto, who had been in Europe when it happened, returned to Santiago

Atitlán to celebrate Mass in honor of the Oklahoma martyr and to pray for him at a memorial Mass.

In his homily, Bishop Melotto said:

> Just five weeks ago on this very altar, together with the Blood of Christ, there was offered in a crystal container, the blood of this Good Shepherd who, the night before, had sacrificed his life for his flock. Those who witnessed that scene would never forget it.... The presence of Father Francisco's blood in this church will be an efficacious sign that will remind coming generations of the great apostolic soul of this priest of Christ. He loved the parish community of Santiago Atitlán with all his heart.

> Those of us who knew and had dealings with Father Francisco Rother will never forget his goodness, his optimism, his generosity, his preoccupation for the poorest and those who suffered most. Many of us who are present here today can testify that Father Francisco really was the Good Shepherd, according to the image painted for us by Christ himself.... Certainly Father Francisco knew his sheep, and knowing them, loved them, and shepherded them according to their needs. His first preoccupation was to understand the mentality of his parishioners, and to do this he spared no effort to learn the difficult language of his people, Tz'utujil, because it is mainly through the spoken language with all its subtleties that one comes to know the mentality of a people and its culture.

Bishop Melotto spoke of Father Stanley's efforts to bring his flock closer to God by encouraging worship in their native Tz'utujil, by publishing the Tz'utujil prayer book, by respectfully updating and restoring the ancient colonial church building, and by gently caring for the sick. "For all of this," the bishop said, "the night the executioners came to take his life, he could have, with good reason, asked them Jesus' question: 'I have done many works for you to see. For which of these do you wish to kill me?'

"Those who suffer martyrdom in these times will be remembered in history as Martyrs of Human Promotion," concluded the bishop, "because all human beings are made in the image of God and are our brothers in Christ. Brothers and sisters, it won't be long before our Father Francisco will also be recognized by the highest authority of the [C]hurch as a true martyr of Christ, and his feast will be celebrated each year on the day he encountered Christ, the 28th of July."

A Martyr for His People

The word "martyr," whose root is the Greek *martys*, literally meaning "witness," was first used in reference to early Christians who were put to death for their confession of faith. Yet a deeper look at the etymology of the word "martyr" shows that in addition to the familiar understanding, "witness," it also derives from the Sanskrit root *smar*, meaning *to remember*.

Stanley Rother witnessed not only to what he had seen with his eyes but also to what he knew in his heart. He believed, he remembered, and he witnessed with his life — and through his death. And we, the community of faith, remember him in thanksgiving for his witness of faith.

In his first apostolic exhortation, *The Joy of the Gospel*, Pope Francis describes what he calls "evangelizing gestures." Often little and always powerful, these are the acts and attitudes that mark a Christian as a missionary. People like Father Stanley Rother, who "preached" fully this incarnational spirituality in his everyday life, understood the importance of these "evangelizing gestures." Because he understood the Gospel values, not as a set of ideas but an affair of the heart, Father Stanley could take care of the most menial duties with his whole being. Whether listening to someone's pain, fixing a car, changing a diaper, driving someone to the doctor, or shopping for supplies for the mission, he understood the reality of God's presence in each act — and by doing so, he proclaimed the Gospel of love, joy, and hope with his whole being.

To put it another way, Father Stanley came to understand with clarity the importance of "presence." By constantly striving to deliberately be present to the people in front of him, to the needs in front of him, Father Stanley proclaimed a God who lives and suffers with his people. For Father Stanley, the choice to die for his Tz'utujil was a natural extension of the daily choice he made to live for them, and in communion with them. His death was nothing less than a proclamation of God's love for the poor of Santiago Atitlán.

"You can't speak of poverty in the abstract: that doesn't exist," emphasized Pope Francis in a talk with Jesuit high school students. "Poverty is the flesh of the poor Jesus, in that child who is hungry, in the one who is sick, in those unjust social structures.

Go forward, look there upon the flesh of Jesus. But don't let well-being rob you of hope, that spirit of well-being that, in the end, leads you to becoming a nothing in life.... But where do I find hope? In the flesh of Jesus who suffers and in true poverty. There is a connection between the two."[25]

Sister Linda Wanner, S.S.N.D., was not only there on the day of Father Stanley's death, but she has also returned to the village for anniversary Masses and to accompany pilgrims to Santiago Atitlán. "Over the years the word 'martyr' and the word 'saint' were naturally used when speaking of the bravery he exhibited in protecting his flock," she said, "like a protector," a role he played in life, and now in death. His death "transformed the village of Santiago Atitlán, pulling it together." During her 10 years as a Guatemala missionary, Sister Linda said she began praying for his intercession, "I asked Stan to intercede for Greg and John [the priests at the parish]. I just believed."

Author Henri Nouwen wrote about his experience visiting Santiago Atitlán three years after Father Stanley's death. "Stan was killed because he was faithful to his people in their long and painful struggle for human dignity," dying not for an abstract cause or an issue, but for his people, in whom he recognized the face of the suffering Lord. "[Stan] stood with them as they learned how to read and write, sought proper nutrition and health care for their children, struggled to acquire small pieces of land to cultivate, and gradually freed themselves from the chains of poverty and oppression."[26] His martyrdom needs to be told, for "martyrs are blood witnesses of God's inexhaustible love for his people."[27] Ultimately, Nouwen wrote, we honor martyrs because they are signs of hope for the living Church, they are reminders of God's loving presence.[28]

With the assistance and endorsement from the Church of Guatemala, the Archdiocese of Oklahoma City concluded the archdiocesan phase of the canonization process in July of 2010, sending Father Stanley Rother's cause to the Congregation for the Causes of Saints in Rome.

As of the writing of this book, the congregation has affirmed the "juridic validity" of the case for Servant of God Stanley Rother. On September 3, 2014, Dr. Andrea Ambrosi, official Relator for the Cause, together with Oklahoma City Archbishop Paul Coakley, presented the *Positio* (or Position Paper) on Father Stanley's martyrdom to the Prefect of the Congregation for the Causes of Saints in Rome.

The *Positio* is being studied by the members of the congregation, who then will recommend to the Holy Father whether Father Stanley Rother can be justly honored as a martyr for the faith. It will be up to Pope Francis to make the ultimate judgment regarding Father Stanley's martyrdom.

Once the Holy Father affirms that Father Stanley Rother died a martyr, permission will be granted for his immediate beatification. Martyrs — those who died for their faith — can be beatified without evidence of a miracle. Father Stanley Rother would then be on his way to potentially becoming the first male saint born in the United States.

But his people in Santiago Atitlán don't need an official declaration. They already affirm Padre Apla's as a saint, *their* saint, and they come to him daily asking for help and intercession — much as they did during the 13 years he served as their priest.

The utility room where Father Stan was martyred is now a small chapel within the rectory courtyard where parishioners gather to pray. The hole left by the bullet is still in the floor. The stain caused by Father Stan's blood is now encased in glass with a hand-written sign: "*SANGRE DE APLA'S, EL 28 DE JU-LIO DE 1,981.*"[29] And in two glass cabinets on the chapel's side wall, some of Father Stan's personal things: the Mass lectionary, photos, his worn-out blue "Co-op seed" cap, certificates given to him by various parish organizations, and stoles.

For the Tz'utujil, Father Stan's death is just one more outward sign of Apla's deep and abiding holy love for them. "He was a courageous missionary, who in spite of the violence that surrounded him, did not leave his flock. He is a great example for me, someone who gave his life for the People of God," explained Sister Ambrosia, a member of the *Hermanas Misioneras de la Eucaristía* (Missionary Sisters of the Eucharist), who remembers and survived the years of violent social unrest in Guatemala.

What Father Stanley wanted was for the people of Santiago Atitlán to make progress, for their "dignity to be respected, to have a chance at education, a chance for the essentials of life — water, food, and medical care," Archbishop Salatka noted. Yet the Guatemalan government needed for the status quo to remain. "They wanted them to be totally dependent, available to work on the fincas.... Stan was conscious of what he was doing. He wasn't out to throw his life away.... Blessed are they who hunger and thirst for justice ... if pursuing his causes meant giving up his life, he would do it."

"I can't tell you how much I admire him. He could have returned to his country, but instead he remained with his people here. He represents Jesus," Sister Ambrosia emphasized, "who gave his life for all of us." Without hesitation, Sister Ambrosia concluded, "All of Guatemala already knows that he is a saint."

Next to the entrance to the historic parish church hangs a large photo banner above the altar where his heart and blood are now entombed, with a vista of the lake and the image of Father Stanley celebrating Mass, along with the words proclaimed by Jesus, "*No hay amor mas grande el que da la vida por sus amigos*" (there is no greater love than this: to lay down one's life for one's friends — cf. Jn 15:13).

"Stanley Rother, in my estimation, had taken on so much of the beauty of Jesus Christ and His strength and gentility that his death was a final act of real transformation," concluded his seminary friend Archbishop Harry J. Flynn.

"From the Beginning of Our Priesthood"

In 1959, five days into his second semester of Theology I at the seminary, 23-year-old Stanley was told he had failed the previous semester and was sent home. That same year, Pope John XXIII published an encyclical titled *Sacerdotii Nostri Primordia* ("From the Beginning of Our Priesthood"), describing the life of St. John Vianney as a model for priests and seminarians.

Several of Father Stanley's friends and teachers immediately saw a spiritual connection between St. John Vianney, the *Curé d'Ars*, and Father Stanley Rother, a connection they likely first noted because of the French saint's own struggles with academics. Yet the parallels between the two priests run much deeper.

Jean-Baptiste-Marie Vianney (May 8, 1786-August 4, 1859), commonly known in English as St. John Vianney, was born into a farm family of devoted Catholics, much like Stanley Rother's German-Catholic Okarche roots. Like Stanley, John's deepest desire as a teenager was to be a priest — yet he struggled with advanced studies, especially Latin. And so, like Stanley, he was sent home from the major seminary (at Lyons). Yet despite being considered "too slow," St. John Vianney had a mentor who defended his vocation to the priesthood. Abbé Bailey believed in John Vianney and encouraged him to persevere. There's even a story of Abbé Bailey persuading the diocese's vicars general that John Vianney's piety and devotion was great enough to compensate for his academic ignorance — a story that echoes Stanley's meeting with his Okarche pastor and Oklahoma's Bishop Reed after failing theology at the San Antonio seminary.

Pope St. John XXIII wrote in his encyclical about St. John Vianney:

> Men in Sacred Orders should gain an adequate knowledge of human affairs and a thorough knowledge of sacred doctrine that is in keeping with their abilities. Would that all pastors of souls would exert as much effort as the Cure of Ars did to overcome difficulties and obstacles in learning, to strengthen memory through practice, and especially to draw knowledge from the Cross of Our Lord, which is the greatest of all books. This is why his Bishop made this reply to some of his critics: "I do not know whether he is learned; but a heavenly light shines in him." (n. 78)

So, too, for Stanley Francis Rother.

St. John Vianney was 29 years old when he was ordained a priest; Stanley Rother was 28. For both men, their life vocation was living and working in a small village where they became champions for the poor, especially children. And the ministry of both men included opening a school in their villages to educate the children.

Father John Vianney struggled to be a pastor to his people in the midst of religious ignorance and indifference after the French Revolution. Father Stanley Rother was the shepherd to a people socially forgotten in Guatemalan culture, who had lived without a resident Catholic priest for almost a century.

Like John Vianney, Stanley Rother's generous service routinely included maneuvering budgets and even selling things, like his own clothes, to donate to charity for the people he served. John Vianney fed the orphans of his village. Stanley Rother fed the widows and fatherless children of his own village.

In this context of service and mission, it is impossible to not think of Stanley Rother alongside John Vianney, who was described the "meekest and humblest of souls" when he was named patron of "all pastors, to promote their spiritual welfare throughout the world," and who "lived in the Church in such a way that he worked for it alone, and burned himself up like a piece of straw being consumed on fiery coals" (nn. 3 and 33).

Pope John XXIII could have been describing Father Stanley Rother's devotion to the Mass when he wrote:

[W]hat is the main point of his apostolate if not seeing to it that wherever the Church lives, a people who are joined by the bonds of faith, regenerated by holy

Baptism and cleansed of their faults will be gathered together around the sacred altar? It is then that the priest, using the sacred power he has received, offers the divine Sacrifice in which Jesus Christ renews the unique immolation which He completed on Calvary for the redemption of mankind and for the glory of His heavenly Father.... There it is that the people of God are taught the doctrines and precepts of faith and are nourished with the Body of Christ, and there it is that they find a means to gain supernatural life, to grow in it, and if need be to regain unity. And there besides, the Mystical Body of Christ, which is the Church, grows with spiritual increase throughout the world down to the end of time. (n. 53)

And instead of St. John Vianney, Pope John XXIII could have been describing Stanley Rother and his faithful ministry to the people of Santiago Atitlán as he emphasized this:

He proved to be a tireless worker for God, one who was wise and devoted in winning over young people and bringing families back to the standards of Christian morality, a worker who was never too tired to show an interest in the human needs of his flock, one whose own way of life was very close to theirs and who was prepared to exert every effort and make any sacrifice to establish Christian schools and to make missions available to the people: and all of these things show that St. John M. Vianney reproduced the true image of the good shepherd in himself as he dealt with the flock entrusted to his care, for he knew his sheep, protected them from dangers, and gently but firmly looked after them. (n. 63)

Priests often find themselves in difficult circumstances, the pope noted. This is not surprising,

> for those who hate the Church always show their hostility by trying to harm and deceive her sacred ministers ... those who want to overthrow religion always try in their hatred to strike at priests first of all.... But even in the face of these serious difficulties, priests who are ardent in their devotion to God enjoy a real, sublime happiness from an awareness of their own position, for they know that they have been called by the Divine Savior to offer their help in a most holy work, which will have an effect on the redemption of the souls of men and on the growth of the Mystical Body of Christ. (nn. 112, 113)

In a coincidence that seems both humorous and providential, Pope John XXIII concludes his 1959 encyclical with a prayer, that throughout the world, the French *Curé d'Ars* "will stir up the pious zeal of priests and of those whom God is calling to take up the priesthood" (n. 119), a prayer that undoubtedly graced dismissed seminarian Stanley Rother that year.

In the words of Pope John XXIII: "How could anyone help being moved deeply with a life so completely dedicated to Christ shining so clearly there before him?" (n. 80).

Father Stanley Rother:
Patron for All Priests

Five years to the day of Stanley Rother's martyrdom, a newly ordained priest, Padre Clemente Peneleu, celebrated Mass in the ancient church of Santiago Atitlán. Father David Monahan described the historic event:

> The wooden casket — made for Stanley Rother and used at funeral Masses for him in Guatemala, but unacceptable for transfer of the body to the United States — sat in the middle aisle of the church in front of the altar. Padre Peneleu's face reflected a bronze sheen framed in jet-black hair. He is a full-blooded Tz'utujil Mayan, the first such to be ordained to the Catholic priesthood. Stanley Rother had befriended the younger Peneleu, once hauling a gift typewriter over the rocky road to Peneleu's home in San Pedro on the other side of the San Pedro volcano. Speaking with great poise and confidence, Father Peneleu declared he offered his entire priesthood to God in honor of Padre Apla's.[30]

By any account, Stanley Francis Rother was a faith-filled, dedicated, purposeful, compassionate, strong-minded man who knew from a young age that he was called to be an ordained minister and follower of Jesus. "Stan had the kind of sanctity that I think should be and could be a model to us, in day-to-day living," Father Gregory Schaffer emphasized. "The *Curé d'Ars* is one of the images I always had of Stan, that kind of spirituality, that kind of prayerfulness in his life ... nothing showy."

In the words of Archbishop Salatka, Father Stanley's life and death "is a sterling example of a willingness to sacrifice." Ultimately, he shaped the Church both in Oklahoma and Guatemala, in that he "made us more willing to give of ourselves ... a deepening of our own faith." Father Stanley Rother is the "good shepherd who gave his life as our Lord did."

It is true that the Church has always depended on the lives of holy men and women to renew the People of God. Yet at this moment in history, the darkness and sin manifested in the clergy abuse scandal of recent years continue to damage the image of the priesthood, threatening to discourage and dissuade some who are being called. It is by God's providence that Stanley Rother lived when he did, at a time when, perhaps more than ever, we need a zealous witness to what the priesthood is — and what it can be.

"Father Stan's devotion to his parishioners, even to the point of laying down his life, shows how all priests are called to make Christ present daily, in their lives and in their ministry," Oklahoma City Archbishop Paul S. Coakley emphasized. "Father Stanley Rother's life, his death, and his witness, are of great consequence not only for the Church in Guatemala and the Church of Oklahoma — but for the Universal Church."

Time and God's providence will tell whether Father Stanley will join St. John Vianney as patron of parish priests. Or perhaps he will become a patron of missions, along with Francis Xavier and Thérèse of Lisieux. What a perfect legacy of love that would be!

Regardless of how he is eventually recognized, Stanley Francis Rother was a faithful man who dared to love Jesus with everything he had — and that changed everything. To paraphrase what G. K. Chesterton wrote of St. Thomas More: If there had not been that particular man at that particular moment, our Church and history would have been different.

Not only because of Father Stanley's death as a martyr. But even more significantly, because his life and his priestly service remain a testament to the difference that one person can, and does, make.

In the words of Archbishop Coakley, "We need the witness of holy men and women who remind us that we are all called to holiness — and that holy men and women come from ordinary places like Okarche, Oklahoma."

EPILOGUE

At the age of 43, one is not prone to look back over the past. At the age of 80, one cannot help but look back to recall and recognize the countless people who have been a positive force in one's long life. In my case, the person of the Servant of God, Father Stanley Rother, stands out. What an inspiration, example, and model.

On April 20, 1978, I was ordained as the bishop of Tulsa. One of the first revelations I discovered was the joint effort with the Archdiocese of Oklahoma City as we shared in sponsoring the mission of Santiago Atitlán in Guatemala. The Oklahoma establishment of this mission went back a little over a full decade. By 1978, much of the original enthusiastic response from Oklahoma had declined. No longer was there a staff of priests, sisters, and laypeople at Santiago Atitlán. The sole Oklahoma representative was Father Stanley Rother, the farm boy from Okarche.

Father Rother had been ordained a priest for the Diocese of Oklahoma City and Tulsa. When Tulsa became a separate diocese in 1973, Father Rother, who was already assigned and ministering in Guatemala, remained a priest of the Archdiocese of Oklahoma City.

However, the first bishop of Tulsa, Bernard J. Ganter, and Archbishop John R. Quinn of Oklahoma City agreed that the two dioceses would continue their mutual collaboration of sponsoring the mission of Santiago Atitlán. Therefore, very soon

after my arrival in Tulsa, Father Rother came for our first meeting to bring me up-to-date on the mission.

I was thrilled to meet this young, zealous, humble Oklahoma missionary. His demeanor was most captivating. He was
a man of integrity, a dedicated missionary who loved God and
his people.

To listen to Father Rother's description of the mission and
his ministry there was so refreshing. The Church was truly alive
under his pastorate. Together with the dedicated leaders whom
he trained and directed, the Word of God was proclaimed,
taught, and lived. Religious education was greatly emphasized
but was not the only ministry of the parish. As a true missionary,
he recognized the material poverty of the people and worked
hard to alleviate it. He loved to visit the families in their homes
and share in their humble lives. He also reached out to the wider
community with a network of social services.

Hearing Father Rother describe his mission life and activity
moved me to express an urgent desire to visit the mission soon.
However, Father Rother cautioned me to wait until the brewing
local tension eased. Unfortunately, a few years later that tension
increased to direct threats on his life, which brought him back
to Oklahoma for a short time. On that occasion, he expressed
such an ardent plea to return to Guatemala to be with his people
that I just had to agree with him. To express my agreement, I
bestowed a very special blessing on him. Then after he left my
office, I called Archbishop Salatka to encourage him to allow
Father Rother to return to Santiago Atitlán, and indeed he did.

From my initial meeting in 1978 until Father Rother's martyrdom in 1981, a priestly bond of love and respect marked our
relationship. That bond of love and respect and admiration in-

creased even more when Father Rother gave up his life for God and for his people. Indeed, as Jesus is the Good Shepherd, so also was Stan "the shepherd who did not run away."

Not long after Father Rother's death, Archbishop Salatka and I met with Bishop Angélico Melotto of the Diocese of Sololá. We met him in Guatemala City, then traveled with him to Santiago Atitlán. At that time, we had already begun speaking about Father Rother's "martyrdom" and urged Bishop Melotto to begin the cause for canonization.

Upon our arrival in Santiago Atitlán, large crowds of people gathered at the church and in the plaza. Much like at the death of St. John Paul II, the people clamored for Father Rother's recognition as a saint. They were convinced of his sanctity.

They revered his heart, which they entombed behind the altar. In later years, his heart was transferred to a beautiful shrine just inside the church entrance. There the people continue even today to approach the enshrined heart of Father Rother with respect, devotion, and love. They bring their requests and pray to him with great confidence because they know that he is indeed a Saint of God.

Almost three and a half decades have passed since Father Rother's death. His life and his death have left a permanent impact on me and on countless other people. He is a constant reminder to me that we are all on a pilgrimage of faith. We enjoy good days and experience some not so good. Father Rother has been a reminder to me that as a bishop (shepherd) I, too, cannot run away but must (even though retired) continue faithfully to walk joyfully in this vale of tears. As St. Augustine expressed this theme so well: "O Lord, our hearts are restless until they find rest in you."

Father Stanley Rother was a very ordinary person. By his life and witness, he showed us that ordinary people can become saints. In fact, all of us are created for that purpose. Stan attained this goal by his ordinary daily dedication to our Lord. Whether in a parish here in Oklahoma or at the mission of Santiago Atitlán, he brought people to recognize the goodness and mercy of God. Through the celebration of the sacraments, the preaching of the Gospel, the sharing of time and compassion, Stanley Rother served as a faithful, humble priest of Jesus Christ. It was to this Lord Jesus that he led his people. It is to this Lord Jesus that Stan now directs us. This was the goal of Father Rother's life and should be the goal of our lives. Jesus and Jesus alone is our Lord and Savior.

Since Father Rother was an Oklahoman and a priest of the Archdiocese of Oklahoma City, we have a special appreciation of his life and death. When his cause for canonization did not materialize in Guatemala, we received permission to initiate the cause here. During this time, prayers for his canonization were offered not only in Oklahoma but throughout the country. The Father Rother Guild continues to foster prayer that the Church Universal will soon proclaim Father Rother a Saint of God. Let us all pray for the canonization of Father Stanley Rother, priest and martyr.

MOST REVEREND EUSEBIUS J. BELTRAN
Archbishop Emeritus of Oklahoma City

NOTES

1. November 29, 2013, meeting of Pope Francis with the Union of Superior Generals in Rome.

2. Letter of December 1980 in David Monahan (ed.), *The Shepherd Cannot Run: Letters of Stanley Rother, Missionary and Martyr* (Oklahoma City: Archdiocese of Oklahoma City, 2010), p. 56. The original wording (including grammar and spelling) of Stanley Rother's writings has been retained for this book.

3. María Ruiz Scaperlanda, *Edith Stein: St. Teresa Benedicta of the Cross* (Huntington, IN: Our Sunday Visitor, 2001), p. 24.

4. Pope Francis, Vatican Radio, October 14, 2013.

5. David Monahan, "Biography of Father Stanley Francis Rother," unpublished manuscript, p. 39.

6. Ibid., p. 45.

7. Ibid., p. 58.

8. Ibid., p. 59.

9. Ibid., pp. 62-63.

10. Ibid., p. 71.

11. Ibid., pp. 72-73.

12. Father John J. Considine, M.M., "Latin America was Major Concern," *Arkansas Catholic* (June 7, 1963), p. 12. Online posting.

13. Barbara E. Verchot, "The Altarpiece of Santiago Atitlán: The 'Flowering Earth Mountain' " (University of Central Florida, unpublished manuscript, c. 2008), p. 6. Online posting.

14. Monahan, "Biography," p. 102.

15. Ibid., pp. 129, 130.

16. Ibid., p. 132.

17. Jeanne Devlin, *Sooner Catholic* (August 12, 2001), "Father Ramon Carlin Larger Than Life: A Priest of the People," p. 7. Online posting.

18. Monahan, "Biography," p. 145.

19. Ibid., p. 166.

20. United Nations, "Guatemala: Memoria de Silencio," Comisión para el Esclarecimiento Histórico (CEH). Vol. VII, Casos Ilustrativos Anexo I. *Caso Ilustrativo No. 11*, pp. 261-265.

21. Ibid.

22. Ibid.

23. Allen J. Christenson, *Arts and Society in a Highland Maya Community: The Altarpiece of Santiago Atitlán* (Austin, TX: University of Texas Press, 2001), pp. 66-67.

24. Bernice Kita, M.M., *What Prize Awaits Us: Letters from Guatemala* (Maryknoll, NY: Orbis Books, 1988), pp. 190-191.

25. Pope Francis, Meeting with Students of Jesuit Schools — Q&A, June 7, 2013.

26. Henri Nouwen, *Love in a Fearful Land: A Guatemalan Story* (Maryknoll, NY: Orbis Books, 2006), pp. 32-33.

27. Nouwen, p. 18.

28. Nouwen, p. 89.

29. The comma between "1" and "9" is in the original text on the sign.

30. Monahan, "Biography," pp. 298–299.

List of Works Consulted

Amnesty International U.S.A., *Testimony on Guatemala*, Amnesty International (July 30, 1981).

Así Empezó Todo ... Historia de la Inglesia con enfasis en Guatemala, Audiovisuales Educativos, 1988.

Beecroft, Nelson, "Making the Case for Martyrdom," *This Land Press* (December 16, 2014). Online posting.

Christenson, Allen J., *Arts and Society in a Highland Maya Community: The Altarpiece of Santiago Atitlán* (Austin, TX: University of Texas Press, 2001).

Considine, Father John J., M.M., "Latin America was Major Concern," *Arkansas Catholic* (June 7, 1963), p. 12. Online posting.

De la Haba, Louis, "Guatemala, Maya and Modern," *National Geographic* (November 1974), pp. 661-689. Online posting.

Devlin, Jeanne, "Father Ramon Carlin Larger Than Life: A Priest of the People," *Sooner Catholic* (August 12, 2001), pp. 7. Online posting.

"Father Stanley Rother, Servant of God: Farmer, Priest, Missionary, Martyr," *Extension* (Christmas 2012), pp. 19-21.

Gilliland, Pat, "Priest Honored 10 Years After Death in Guatemala," *Saturday Oklahoman & Times* (July 27, 1991), p. 10.

Greenhalgh, Kurt, and Mark Gruenke, F.S.C., eds., *The Church Martyred: Guatemala*. No publisher listed, c.1981.

"Guatemala: Requiem for a Missionary," *Time* (August 10, 1981). Online posting.

Henninger, Dan. "Two New Saints. Now What?" *Wall Street Journal* (April 23, 2014).

Hiding, Alan, "Guatemala: State of Siege," *New York Times* (August 24, 1980), p. 16. Online posting.

——, "Political Killings Widen In Guatemala, The Middle Is No Sanctuary," *New York Times* (June 15, 1980), p. E3. Online posting.

Hinton, Carla, "Locals seek sainthood for martyred priest," *The Oklahoman* (July 17, 2010), pp. 1D, 3D.

Jackson, Ron, "nDepth Stories of the Ages: The Shepherd Who Didn't Run," *NewsOK* (no date). Online posting.

Jensen, Derrick, "Saving the Indigenous Soul: An Interview With Martín Prechtel," *The Sun* (April 2001). Online posting.

Kita, Bernice, M.M., *What Prize Awaits Us: Letters from Guatemala* (Maryknoll, NY: Orbis Books, 1988).

——, "They Killed Stan," *Maryknoll Magazine* (November 2006), pp. 38–40.

Marden, Luis, "To Market in Guatemala," *National Geographic* (July 1945), pp. 87–104. Online posting.

Monahan, David, "Biography of Father Stanley Francis Rother," unpublished manuscript.

——, ed., *The Shepherd Cannot Run: Letters of Stanley Rother, Missionary and Martyr* (Oklahoma City: Archdiocese of Oklahoma City, 2010).

——, "All night vigil, people's hunger moved McSherry to volunteer," *Sooner Catholic* (July 1, 1984), p. 3.

——, "Three years after killing, priests return to mission," *Sooner Catholic* (June 3, 1984), p. 1.

Nouwen, Henri. *Love in a Fearful Land: A Guatemalan Story* (Maryknoll, NY: Orbis Books, 2006).

"Padre Francis Stanley Rother, Presbítero," *Testigos fieles del Evangelio*, Conferencia Episcopal de Guatemala (March 2007), pp. 375-382.

Pope Francis, apostolic letter, "To All Consecrated People on the Occasion of the Year of Consecrated Life" (November 21, 2014). Online posting.

——, "Pope Francis: imitate martyrs, don't be 'painted' Christians," Vatican Radio (October 14, 2013). Online posting.

Pope St. John XXIII, *Sacerdotii Nostri Primordia* ("From the Beginning of Our Priesthood," on St. John Vianney) (August 1, 1959). Online posting.

Quezada, Ariana, " 'A Joyful Privileged Burden': The Life of Father Stanley Rother," *The Chronicles of Oklahoma* (Spring 2012), pp. 28-51.

Ramirez, Cruz, *Stanley Rother's Life and Martyrdom*, unpublished essay, 2007.

Rojas Lima, Flavio, "La cofradía indigena, reducto cultural de los mayas de Guatemala," *Sociedad Española de Estudios Mayas* (1986), pp. 253-282. Online posting.

Romeri, Gabriela, "Guatemala: Struggling from Genocide to Justice," *Maryknoll Magazine* (December 2013), pp. 50-54.

Rosengreen, John, "Father Stan Rother: American Martyr in Guatemala," *St. Anthony Messenger* (July 2006).

Scaperlanda, María Ruiz, *Edith Stein: St. Teresa Benedicta of the Cross* (Huntington, IN: Our Sunday Visitor, 2001).

——, "Martyr's Crown," *North Texas Catholic* (November 2011), pp. 32, 24-25.

——, "No Greater Love: No Greater Sacrifice," *Our Sunday Visitor* (November 27, 2011), pp. 18-19.

——, Interview with Father David Monahan, unpublished (October 12, 2004).

——, "A Celebration of the Love, Life of Father Rother: Pilgrims Mark Anniversary," *Sooner Catholic* (September 11, 2011), pp. 11-15.

Smith, Griffin, Jr., "Guatemala: A Fragile Democracy," *National Geographic* (June 1988), pp. 769-802. Online posting.

"Statement on Central America," United States Conference of Catholic Bishops (November 19, 1981). Online posting.

United Nations, "Guatemala: Memoria de Silencio," Comisión para el Esclarecimiento Histórico (CEH), Vol. VII, Casos Ilustrativos Anexo I. *Caso Ilustrativo No. 11.*

Verchot, Barbara E., "The Altarpiece of Santiago Atitlán: The 'Flowering Earth Mountain' " (University of Central Florida, unpublished manuscript, c. 2008). Online posting.

ACKNOWLEDGMENTS

The last time I saw Father David Monahan in person he and I laughed a lot. We laughed remembering his growing up in Tulsa, his family, and "being a mean little kid." And we laughed a great deal as he told me stories, often self-deprecating, about his early years as a priest, as well as many memories of the priests who mentored and encouraged his vocation.

"The best way to have vocations is to have good priests," I remember Father Monahan explaining, with a smile. "Me? I just hope I didn't run anybody off," he added, letting out a big belly laugh.

It was typical Father Monahan. No matter how frustrated he must have been about his mind "slipping" and about the condition increasingly claiming his life and memories, he never allowed hopelessness to affect his attitude — or his sense of humor.

Ultimately, it is his "mind slipping" that is to blame for not allowing Father Monahan to complete and publish the book that became his life passion — the first extensive and detailed biography of Father Stanley Francis Rother, a fellow priest and friend, whom he deeply admired.

Although he never read this book, I owe a mountain of gratitude to Father Monahan for his guidance in this book project. In spite of it being unpublished, his thorough manuscript provided me a detailed map I could always trust for accuracy. And as I poured over boxes of archival material, interviews, research, history, and background on Father Stanley's life, much of it collected and classified by him, I counted on Father Monahan's prayers and guidance from heaven.

To Father David Francis Monahan I owe a grateful and profound tribute of praise.

I am particularly grateful for the assistance given by Father Stanley's siblings and extended family. Thank you, Tom and Marti Rother, and Sister Marita Rother, for welcoming me into your life and for your willingness to share with me your experiences and memories of your extraordinary brother.

My special thanks to Archbishop Paul S. Coakley for allowing me the honor of working on this inspiring project, and to the many dedicated Church personnel who work at the Archdiocese of Oklahoma City's Pastoral Center, who generously offered me one or four extra hands. *Muchas, muchas gracias* George Rigazzi, Cara Koenig, Loutitia Denison Eason, Rosemary Lewis, and Carol Davito.

In addition, many thanks to the Rother family and to the Archdiocese of Oklahoma City for their valuable contribution of personal and archival photos for this book.

I am grateful to Bert Ghezzi, George Foster, Tyler Ottinger, Polly King, and the rest of the editorial and marketing team at Our Sunday Visitor for their vision in publishing and promoting this story of the Martyr from Okarche, Oklahoma.

Finally, my heartfelt thanks to my family for the love, humor, encouragement, and support of this project — my parents, my amazing children, and book-loving grandchildren — and above all, my home editor and husband, Michael. Your enthusiasm gives me energy!

As I said good-bye to Father Monahan that Tuesday afternoon in October 2004, I asked him to pray for me and for my writing project, as is my custom as a writer. I will never forget Father Monahan's reply, one of the most beautiful, honest statements I have ever heard.

"Maria," he looked over at me and smiled, "I'm getting ready to go see God. I'm the one who needs the prayers. Pray for me!"

In this Year of Consecrated Life, I dedicate this powerful story of one devoted priest from Okarche, Oklahoma, to the *many* faithful priests, nuns, brothers, and sisters who have and continue to mold and enrich my life. You are Light!

MAP OF GUATEMALA

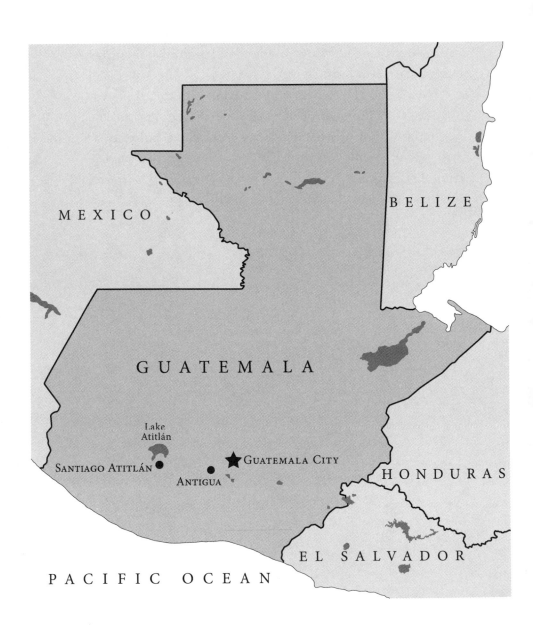